A Cool Customer:
Joan Didion's *The Year of Magical Thinking*
—JACOB BACHARACH

An Oasis of Horror in a Desert of Boredom:
Roberto Bolaño's *2666*
—JONATHAN RUSSELL CLARK

New Uses for Failure:
Ben Lerner's *10:04*
—ADAM COLMAN

A Little in Love with Everyone:
Alison Bechdel's *Fun Home*
—GENEVIEVE HUDSON

I Meant to Kill Ye:
Cormac McCarthy's *Blood Meridian*
—STEPHANIE REENTS

Bizarro Worlds:
Jonathan Lethem's *The Fortress of Solitude*
—STACIE WILLIAMS

BIZARRO WORLDS

Jonathan Lethem's
The Fortress of Solitude

Stacie Williams

FICTION ADVOCATE

New York • San Francisco • Providence

A Fiction Advocate Book

Bizarro Worlds:
Jonathan Lethem's *The Fortress of Solitude*
© 2018 by Stacie Williams
All Rights Reserved

ISBN: 978-0-9994316-2-7

FICTION ADVOCATE
New York • San Francisco • Providence
fictionadvocate.com

Published in the United States of America

CONTENTS

INTRODUCTION

I started telling this story several different times, in different ways. I thought that this was a story about random occurrences, luck or my own tendency toward hard work.

How American of a lie would that have been, especially while attempting to talk about gentrification, and especially through the lens of Jonathan Lethem's 2003 book *The Fortress of Solitude*, which quilts together race, class, hip hop, punk music, gentrification and Brooklyn's Gowanus neighborhood as a means of exploring love, fear and alienation?

I thought that I would be discussing how the lead character—a young white outcast named Dylan—shared some similarities with me but that ultimately my life was harder as a black woman experiencing bigotry or sexism or classism. That while we were joined in the occasional social isolation of our '80s flavored nerditry,

I ultimately sought to build a home and community, while Dylan the rolling stone spends his life running from the implications and privileges of his whiteness. But I realized that those stories, while true and multiple, didn't do enough to reveal my role in a bigger system, or interrogate either Dylan or the semi-autobiographical world that Lethem unfolded for readers.

Gentrification rumbles beneath the narrative like so many subway trains as it charts the Ebdus family's arrival to Gowanus and documents the changing Brooklyn neighborhood over time. *The Fortress of Solitude* vividly illustrates a crumbling 1970s New York City in the throes of white flight and on the edge of bankruptcy, wet with fresh graffiti tags while the discordant sounds of punk and hip hop drifted down city streets. But the stories behind gentrification, or what causes the phenomenon, are things that Lethem through Dylan only skirts around the edges of. He doesn't go much further than what he can see with his eyes. And neither did I for a long time.

We both wandered into the fog of nostalgia, which distorted how we perceived our roles and our complicity within our communities. In his novel *An Unnecessary Woman*, Lebanese-American artist Rabih Alameddine wrote "no nostalgia hurts as much as nostalgia for things that never existed." Nostalgia twists the past into a sepia-colored fiction. We see things not as they are, but as we wanted them to be or wished they never were. Nostalgia dims the ferocity of love or hate through the distance of time. But we can't change the past. And we can't lie about it either.

Gentrification, and conversely *The Fortress of Solitude* are both about what happens when we try to build a future on the bones of nostalgia. It's about what happens when we lie about who we are and what we've always done.

* * * *

In 2003, I had never heard of Jonathan Lethem. But I had heard of the Fortress of Solitude, the name of Superman's secret Arctic lair and also the name of Lethem's book, released that fall. I found the book while browsing at my favorite, now closed, bookstore on the east side of Milwaukee, Harry Schwartz, and reading the back cover, there were keywords that caught my attention: a character named Mingus, which stirred my affinity for jazz music; the 1970s New York setting, which because I considered myself an amateur film buff was already built up in my head with almost mythic significance; the beginnings of hip hop; the comic book homage, as referenced by the title; and a blossoming friendship between two young boys. All of these topics suggested that at a minimum, I would probably like the book even though I hadn't heard of the author, so I took it to the register and paid for it with money left over from a recently cashed unemployment check. I had gotten laid off earlier in the year from my first post-college job as an editorial assistant at an education magazine, and even though I was freelancing regularly, I had a *lot* of spare time, so I read as many books as I could.

The Fortress of Solitude was a page turner. I was fully invested in the evolution of Dylan Ebdus, a geeky white kid living in and navigating a mostly black Brooklyn neighborhood. I could close my eyes and envision Dylan as one of the few white kids in my all-black public elementary or middle schools navigating puberty as a visible minority. As a comic book fan, the Fortress of Solitude concept spoke to me personally: Like Clark Kent, I was a journalist (or trying to be), nerdy and neurotic in my glasses, trying to fit into my adult body and figure out how to use it without hurting anyone or myself, walking through my urban surroundings and wondering how I could use my writing skills to help other people. My apartment at that time was my fortress of solitude; it was a decent-sized studio across town in a mostly Latinx South Side Milwaukee neighborhood where no one knew who I was, and where I could sleep until noon or read books in my Ikea platform bed until it was time to do some writing or meet a source. I felt a kinship with Dylan, who similarly used his childhood home as his hideaway from the stresses of his life: his maternal abandonment, neighborhood bully Robert Woolfolk, burgeoning adolescence, and the dropped-in-from-outer-space feeling of being the only white kid in a mostly black and Latinx neighborhood.

Like the Man of Steel, Dylan and I knew what it meant to be alien in our physical spaces.

As the years went on and I also moved to other cities like Dylan, I came to understand the book as a compelling medium through which to consider gentrification as both a cause and symptom of social issues; it's the sewer of racism and capitalism slushing beneath everything. Gentrification affects the ways we try or fail to build a home and community with each other because it's built on the lie of nostalgia.

Gentrification is a fully but not uniquely American story. It covers many of the issues that have always shaped our society over time: racism, land, and money.

It ultimately rejects authenticity, warping buildings and histories to something unrecognizable. It plays on a tired, false binary of "civilization" vs. "savagery" that people find easy to ignore when it comes paired with artisanal hamburgers and a craft beer. Gentrification is an ultimately doomed phenomenon, fated to cycle between phases of flight, fear, and retrenchment.

Gentrification is also about belonging, about whose lives and histories are included and positively affirmed through policy and local support, and whose are razed and erased.

As a black woman in America, I regularly weave in and out of the borders of belonging. Included here, excluded there, and then moments of ambiguity. For instance, I could say I grew up middle class, but the fact that my college-educated parents had four jobs between them when I was growing up speaks to how slippery that title really is. As an adult creative, like the members of the Ebdus clan, I alternated between times when I was financially comfortable enough to take vacations to other continents, and selling plasma to pay a light bill. I was certainly not as privileged as Mingus—an R&B singer's son with dollar bills scattered around the house like so much confetti who knew that the price of his custody was a cool million dollars.

Dylan and I both spent our youth in pursuit of acceptance. For various reasons, we were ripe targets for bullies. Where Dylan was yoked by his neck, baptized over and over as a *whiteboy*, the kids who picked on me accused me of "talking like a white girl"—I understood later that the insult was more about my know-it-all tone. Where we couldn't find a consistent sense of community among our peers, we dived into books. He had his comic books, I was obsessive about Mildred D. Taylor and Judy Blume, though I did enjoy reading and re-reading the few Marvel comics that my fan father managed to save from his youth. There was solace in the stories of people with strange powers who were frequently ostracized in mainstream society but found community with others like them.

Threading Superman into the title is a sly commentary on the idea of belonging. Kal-El is a quintessential American—a refugee who lands here and has assimilated his authentic self under so many layers that he's never *not* an outsider. The only place that he can be himself is the Fortress of Solitude. He will sit at home alone, looking at archived videos made by his parents in their primary language. Moving through all of these identities is so exhausting for him that he has to be alone with no one around for thousands of miles—the ultimate introvert recharge.

For me, gentrification always comes back to this idea of home. But what does it mean when home is either a reflection or negation of your authentic self? What is home to me as a black woman who shifts through class constructs with static identities of race and gender presentation versus what home means for Dylan, or even that matter, for Superman—two white-presenting males on the outside who also feel like outsiders in their worlds? How do we find our idea of home and keep it authentic as the world outside changes by the millisecond?

How do we tell the truth about ourselves? This book is me trying to tell you the truth, or many truths, about gentrification. About race. About gender. About America and capitalism and what it does to our sense of community and self. I'm using Lethem's book to explore some particularly American ways that we talk about or act out feelings about education, housing, policing, and class in our neighborhoods. How do we tell the truth? We start by first acknowledging it.

PART I

ORIGIN STORIES

———

Origins and Omens
(Superman #685/2)

Every character has an origin story. The concept of gentrification has several origin stories. But in order to fully understand gentrification, it helps to start with the ghetto.

According to writer and historian Riccardo Calimani, the ghetto was originally used to describe an island in Venice, Italy, that was built on a copper foundry: *il geto*[1]. In 1516, city officials forced all of the Jews in the city to live on that island. Segregation and restriction of movement was always a part of the definition and application of the term. Forcing people to live in a certain area was as much about political and economic power as it was hatred and prejudice.

Most people tend to be familiar with ghettos as applied to European Jewish communities in the 1930s and 1940s when Adolf Hitler rose to power in Germany. Jewish citizens across the continent were stripped of their finances, homes, civil rights, and forced into densely packed areas lacking heat or plumbing. Poor living conditions were the point of the ghetto. People were forced to live in a ghetto because they were seen as alien. Inhuman. In many cases, they were jailed in those neighborhoods behind barbed wire fences and occupying soldiers. Some of the neighborhoods became concentration camps or were the site of coordinated acts of terror and mass killings.

That relationship between segregation and slum ties to how the concept of the ghetto would eventually come to include the group of people systematically oppressed since dragged to America in chains in the 17th century: African Americans. In *Ghetto*, author Mitchell Duneier researched archived newspapers before and after World War II and found that while the phrase was only used occasionally before the war to refer to areas where African Americans lived, after World War II, there was a huge spike in the term referring to black neighborhoods. This increase in frequency of the term also corresponded with a rise in mentions of "Warsaw ghettos" or "Jewish ghettos." Editors and news consumers were making or creating through media the connection between the conditions that Jews had been forced to suffer through and those that African Americans were living in across the country.

Before and after the Civil War, black and brown people were always restricted to or away from certain neighborhoods, parts of a city or specific towns. These areas became "ghetto" due to their very association with blacks, without regard to the social and legal constraints forcing such a diverse group of people to stay in those neighborhoods. African Americans who found jobs and wanted to put their income toward their version of the American dream by purchasing a home—especially those who had moved north during the Great Migration—found that they were relegated to certain neighborhoods, violently chased out of white neighborhoods or suburbs, and forced to pay exorbitant amounts of money for limited, substandard housing. In his much-read and discussed 2014 argument for African-American reparations, former *Atlantic Monthly* writer Ta-Nehisi Coates analyzed the outcomes of federal and banking laws that conspired to keep African Americans and other marginalized groups, such as Latinx, Chinese or Southeast Asian communities, tightly packed together in substandard housing in neighborhoods that lacked basic city services and amenities, from the 18th century to the present. This was more than just "unfair." The situation contributed to generations of inequality and poverty and was at times fatal for those forced to endure it. Politicians responded to conditions in the ghettos through aggressive and prejudiced policing, mass incarceration, environmental racism, state and municipal de-investment, and criminalization of poverty, effectively making sure that very few people could escape those circumstances. White people responded by moving into the suburbs, with assistance from the government in the form of military or FHA loans that were denied to African-American citizens.

This history is the source for much of the underlying tension that accompanies gentrification.

The Fortress of Solitude jumps the reader directly into that tension, by beginning the book in the middle of a common scene in gentrifying neighborhoods: two young white girls in nightdresses, they're glimpsed throughout the neighborhood playing freely, chanting children's rhymes. The Solver girls are ghosts who haunt Isabel Vendle's early dreams of turning a neighborhood near a trash-filled canal into a homestead for sophisticated, monied white people. For black and brown people in the neighborhood, the Solver girls' presence strikes a more ominous note.

CHAPTER 1

A STEP BELOW NOBILITY

Understanding the conditions that led to the ghetto helps gives context to the more contemporary display of gentrification in cities. It has always been tied to money. The etymology is related to the word gentry and gentle, which both mean "of high social standing" or "of the upper classes." The gentry as a group were a step below English nobility.

In 1964, British sociologist Ruth Glass coined the term gentrification after witnessing artists and members of the generationally wealthy creative class pushing out lower-income residents in the slums after fixing up the available real estate. Glass studied distribution of wealth through a Marxist lens and built much of her work around the social changes she saw in her own neighborhood in Islington. She noted that capitalism was the guiding force behind the class inequality that created the conditions for gentrification to flourish and also provided the fuel to keep the cycle replaying over and over again. Given that much of her research took place in Britain, it didn't cover the specific way that race asserts itself in American society, though it's worth noting that when the "gentry" landed in Islington, they pushed out large groups of West Indian transplants who had settled into the pre-war buildings. Glass felt strongly that her research and other sociological findings should be used to better other people's lives. Her work on gentrification was as much warning as it was analysis.

In *The Fortress of Solitude*, Dylan's neighbor Isabel Vendle understood that whiteness would get her what she wanted, but it had to be a specific kind of whiteness: whiteness plus financial *and* social privilege. The Ebdus clan was too bohemian for her.

Rachel and Abraham are more like Ruth Glass' idea of the gentry, with more social capital than financial assets, though they can get cash if they need it. They may be part of the "Back to the City" movement of the 1970s, in which small numbers of white people returned to the city and renovated rundown buildings. Yippies, poets, and radical activists are frequent visitors to their home, and they also rent out their basement to other tenants. "Rachel had taught (Dylan) the word *gentrification*. This was a Nixon word, uncool. 'If someone asks you say you live in *Gowanus*,' she said. 'Don't be ashamed. Boerum Hill is pretentious bullshit.'" To Isabel, Rachel is "too Brooklyn"; speaking Spanish to the other neighbors and sending her long-haired folk singer-named son to play scully with the black and brown kids on the block. Abraham's art isn't the "right" kind of art; Isabel finds all the naked paintings of Rachel to be exceptionally tacky.

Lethem describes Rachel as a "Brooklyn street kid," which likely explains why she wanted to remain in the city instead of moving her young family to a whiter or more segregated area. In that way, she's similar to my mom, who grew up riding the subway and playing double dutch with neighborhood girls. My mom, like Rachel Ebdus, preferred to raise her children in an urban space. My sister and I also played double dutch with the neighborhood girls, rode mass transit, and went to public schools.

* * * *

My own origin story is defined by segregation; my personal map stretches from the Midwest to Maine. I was born in Milwaukee, Wisconsin, in the late 1970s, and after college, I moved to Chicago in the early aughts. After several years in Chicago, I went to graduate school in for two years; then moved to Lexington, Kentucky, for nearly four years; and moved to Cleveland, Ohio. My parents were from Chicago, a city that still, in a 21st century of not-quite-flying hoverboards and AI-wired telephones, is terminally segregated by race. Both of them grew up on the South Side, albeit in different class categories, but segregation was the default standard of living. My mom and her friends shuttled across town to the northwest side Edgewater neighborhood to attend a recently desegregated Robert Senn High School in the late 1960s; my dad still remembers being chased out of the Bridgeport neighborhood—home to both mayors Daley—by white teenagers when he was a boy. When my sisters and I visited my maternal grandparents as a young girl, I remember thinking that all of the white people in the city must have lived downtown because I never saw any on 87th Street; I only saw them when we went to the museums or shopping.

Milwaukee was the same. Though my family and I lived in one of the few integrated neighborhoods in the city—with white and black residents, including a large Orthodox Jewish community—Sherman Park was an island on the north side surrounded by all-black neighborhoods, and the neighborhood wasn't even integrated until the early 1980s. My mom still recalls bringing home my youngest sister from the hospital and our German-American next-door neighbor remarked in awe that she "had never seen a colored baby before." The neighborhood was economically homogenous; everyone was working class or middle class, and on our particular street, most of the two-parent households had two working adults.

Milwaukee was one of the final stops for southern black people who had moved north during the Great Migration—the exodus of over six million African Americans escaping domestic terrorism from the south to northern cities like Chicago, Detroit, New York City, Washington, D.C., and Cleveland. By the time black people got to Milwaukee, many of the factory jobs that had propped up the city's working and middle classes were gone, leaving black people disproportionately unemployed and resented by white laborers as competition for scarce jobs—jobs made even harder to find because of rapid deindustrialization. All the factory jobs were going away that had allowed people to buy their neat little two-story cottages and colonials, and states all over the Rust Belt were feeling the same pain: Illinois, Ohio, Pennsylvania, Missouri, Indiana, upstate New York. On the far northwest side of Milwaukee there were mostly white neighborhoods and small suburban villages, but black families made up the North Side inner city. The east side had another racially integrated neighborhood, Riverwest, but that was another island, surrounded by inner-ring suburbs like Shorewood and Whitefish Bay (referred to on the low as "Whitefolks Bay") and affluent neighborhoods adjacent to the University of Wisconsin at Milwaukee. The south side neighborhoods nearest to downtown were mostly Mexican families and the rest of the south side was Eastern European white families, many with Polish roots. Going to high school on the south side was the first time I had ever been around that many white people before, and I was the first black person some of them had seen in real life.

The history of housing in this country indicates that Dylan's family was raised within this same paradigm. His parents, born pre-Civil Rights Movement, probably grew up in segregated white neighborhoods. Rachel's family may have been of the Brooklyn evoked by Betty Smith with large groups of white first- and second-generation immigrants building ethnic enclaves block by block. At some point, Rachel developed her own particular social mobility, evinced in her Spanish fluency and other code switching. At a minimum, Rachel has left the borough and been exposed to other things, though the manner in which she takes leave of her family raises the question as to whether she travels because she's bored by domesticity or because she had always wanted to and never had the opportunity.

Abraham's background is never really explored, possibly because his interactions outside of the house or his artwork are so minimal. He navigates New York like a native; he has a wariness and weariness that suggests he's seen quite a few things, but he doesn't cease to be occasionally shocked by the callousness or carelessness of things one finds in the city. His life before Rachel, including wherever he went to art school, was likely very monochromatic. Abraham loved Rachel and probably agreed to follow her anywhere, even to this more racially mixed neighborhood that he hadn't grown up in. His social awkwardness meant that it didn't matter because he was unlikely to engage those neighbors anyway.

Someone else unlikely to have neighbors over for a backyard barbecue was Barrett Rude Jr. When Barrett makes his way to Gowanus, he does so at a much higher level of economic privilege than anyone else in the neighborhood. He's not from Brooklyn or even New York, so he's not returning as a neighborhood prodigal son. It's unlikely that someone with that level of privilege would have moved to a neighborhood that was still well on the side of working class or low-income at that time. R&B singers of the era tended to live on estates in rural or suburban areas. Members of the O'Jays, for instance, who would've been Barrett's contemporaries, lived in the Cleveland inner-ring suburb of Shaker Heights once they made it. Otis Redding built a ranch estate in Gray, Georgia. Bill Withers still has a home high in the Hollywood Hills. Barrett moving to the neighborhood isn't necessarily in line with historic expectations about how people, black or white, choose to live when they get that kind of money.

Barrett, like Abraham, wasn't really into hanging out with the neighbors anyway, and imported most of his industry friends and lackeys to the neighborhood for his music scene parties. It could have been that Barrett, after divorcing his white wife, wanted to "come home" in a metaphorical sense and be physically near people who looked like him, but where he could be personally anonymous. In that sense, we have something in common.

CHAPTER 2

MIND THE GAP

Where Angels Fear to Tread!
(Luke Cage: Hero for Hire #9)

Lethem positions his story after Glass' definition of gentrification has taken hold in the American cultural imagination. Even though Lethem is about 15 years older than me, the stories of our youth intersect at a specific period in this timeline: the late 1970s through the 1980s. In the 1980s, Ronald Reagan's "Just Say No" to drugs campaign was exacerbating the already growing inequality and disinvestment in city neighborhoods, law enforcement was encouraged to target people of color in a heavily militarized way. The Los Angeles Police Department, for instance started responding to drug raids with war-ready SWAT teams driving tanks and covered in bulletproof armor. Older buildings in these neighborhoods, crumbling from neglect and chopped up into rooming houses, were already suffering from economic neglect brought on by redlining. Some of the iconic brownstones synonymous with Dylan's Brooklyn were at that time being covered with aluminum siding by owners who couldn't afford to or weren't interested in preserving turn-of-the-century bricks.

This 1970s–1980s image of the *inner cities*—the term being used as a dog whistle for ghetto—was mentioned ad nauseum during the 2016 presidential campaign and stands in stark contrast to what many central cities actually look like today. "You're living in hell," then-candidate Donald Trump said about inner cities in an angry, condescending appeal to African Americans during the second of three televised debates in 2016. He seemed to be recalling scenes from the film adaptation of Tom Wolfe's *Bonfire of the Vanities*, with blockades and inexplicable street fires in the hood, and menacing-looking black people doing criminal things in the streets. Or perhaps *New Jack City*, with cackling crackheads on every corner and apartment buildings turned into drug distribution centers. Trump, in his boldly racist appeal to "make America great again" seemed to be nostalgic for 1980s-era pop culture heros: white male titans of industry. Greed was good, according to politicians who codified deep tax cuts for the wealthy. Trump's vision of the inner city is haunted by the specter of the Central Park Jogger— Tricia Meili, a young white woman who was brutally raped and beaten in 1989 while jogging in the park. Trump took out a full-page ad in the *New York Times* at the time, demanding the death penalty for the five young African-American boys wrongly convicted of the assault.[2]

I was born at the tail end of the 1970s; in the 1980s, my fellow elementary school peers and I were rehearsing D.A.R.E[3] songs for school assemblies. Dylan and Mingus were drifting from each other as the latter's drug and alcohol use hardened in tandem with Barrett's addiction; he was smoking crack like so many others at that time. I attended a public school in a neighborhood where it was not uncommon to see crack vials or paraphernalia on the playground, but it was also a magnet school similar to Stuyvesant High School, which Dylan attended in the book. Growing up, Dylan and I saw a lot of the same things, though I was far too young to make sense out of any of it. We were still both trying to figure out how to be our authentic selves while at school.

Among the mostly white students into whose gifted and talented groups I'd been tracked, I didn't fit in. My clothes weren't cool enough, I couldn't quite perfect the denim ankle fold everyone was rocking and I didn't have any of the fashionable elementary-age accoutrements advertised on television—Trapper Keepers, fun erasers, stickers—that the white kids in my section used to determine cool. I only listened to the radio, and while I was fluent in Michael Jackson, Madonna, Prince and Paula Abdul, I didn't have the knowledge about edgier bands or groups that my class-mates' older siblings passed down to them. I started wearing glasses in third grade, which invited procla-mations of "Four Eyes," and I was painfully awkward. I talked too much or too loud at the wrong times, other times I was quiet when I should have been joining in. I wasn't from the neighborhood the school was located in and it was clear there was a class divide, but those things went over my head at the time. I was probably performing certain things and doing it in a know-it-all or snobby way (see: "talk like a white girl") and not realizing it, further marking me as different. Ignored by one group, bullied by another, such was life. I coped by trying to spend lunch hours and recess times in the library where I could read *Blubber* in peace.

Dylan, in contrast, had Mingus to open doors of friendship to him. Mingus was the buffer between Dylan and bully Robert Woolfolk, was Dylan's dimension to alternate galaxies populated by Avengers, hip-hop royalty, and tagging crews. How did Dylan repay the friendship that I would have eagerly accepted if it had been offered? He started avoiding Mingus and Dean Street in general.

By middle school, he had found a new group of mostly white friends, nerds like him who were even bigger outsiders, but cool, by dint of their residence on Roosevelt Island. Instead of geeking out on the latest blaxploitation movie or *Avengers* comics, his new source of pop cultural context became very white. "Steve Martin and Marty Feldman and George Carlin, Devo, Python, Zappa, Spock, *The Prisoner*," Lethem wrote. His friends are into punk. Dylan appropriates the identity, and it's like an ill-fitting motorcycle jacket—nothing he can get comfortable in. Lethem creates a poignant scene—switching perspective to Dylan's inner voice in the second person—where Dylan tries to rationalize the cavalier way his friends make fun of the hip-hop classic "Rapper's Delight." He even recognizes that his friends' reactions to the album are racist and being where he's from, he knows how important the album is. He knows who he's betraying by not acknowledging this. But like all teens, he wants to fit in and wants not to care so much about it. "That's a small price to pay for growing up, isn't it?" Lethem asks in Dylan's inner consciousness.

From that point, Dylan emotionally and physically began to break from home. He spent as much time as he could with his high school friends; on Dean Street he holed away in his room. In a single afternoon, the connection to his Dean Street fortress was irreversibly changed forever, and he left the neighborhood for a fresh start in college, spending the rest of the novel unmoored and suffering a blend of guilt and relief about having left.

By the time I was in high school, I wanted to leave too. I wanted out of Sherman Park, out of Wisconsin. Given that my family was not originally from Milwaukee, I didn't necessarily feel the same kind of generational tie to the city that many of my friends did. When the time came to consider college, I found out, according to FAFSA anyway, I was in a weird not-poor-but-too-middle-class to qualify for any grants or scholarships category, which narrowed my out-of-state options considerably.

Compounding that, my senior year of high school was the same year my dad had been laid off from the bank. I had a sister 13 months younger who would be heading to college right after me. Madison, Wisconsin, a mere 90 minutes away, was as far away as I could afford to go. I was fortunate in that my grandmother and parents paid for my college expenses, however, the phrase "mind the gap," is incredibly relevant.

Though my grandmother and my parents graduated from college, they all received scholarships—my father started with a scholarship and ended with the G.I. bill after being drafted during the Vietnam War—at a time when the costs of attending college at a public university were extremely low. We were all unprepared for the sticker shock of 1990s college costs, and the on-campus jobs I was working couldn't keep up. For instance, UW-Madison had no dorm meal plans; everything was paid for a la carte and by the weight. Despite starting school with healthy intentions, I learned quickly that I couldn't load my bowls up with pineapple and watermelon or pasta. My parents accused me freshman year of taking money they sent for food and spending it on clothes. I couldn't convince them otherwise and they stopped sending money that semester. My friends who were first-generation college students with much better aid packages would call my room when it was time to eat and buy food for me from their accounts. Knowing the situation at home, I tried not to call if I could help it. My parents were leveraging things I couldn't even have known about to try and assist when they could on the larger expenses of books and board for their first-born kid.

Mind the gap.

Some of Dylan's and my college experiences dovetailed: We both spent time working in the campus cafeteria, we both threw ourselves into alternative media—radio for him, campus magazine for me— as a means of expressing ourselves and our passions. However, Dylan attended (fictional) affluent liberal arts Camden College in Vermont, where I went to a state school, so I hadn't (yet) been exposed to the cultural class shock that he experienced.[4] Most of my friends were from the same working- or middle-class backgrounds that had the been standard I saw growing up.

Dylan broke his ties to New York after college. I, on the other hand, finished my journalism degree, and then I had to move back to my parents' house, sharing a room with my two sisters because I couldn't find a job. A month after I returned home, two planes sliced through giant steel towers in New York City like molten swords. I spent two more months filling out applications at the mall before I was hired at a nationally-distributed progressive education magazine. One of my first editorial tasks involved searching for photographs documenting September 11, 2001: the towers that fell, and ash-dusted people trudging across the Brooklyn Bridge back to their homes.

As journalists, Dylan and I probably had very similar social lives. I worked for several alt-weekly newspapers and web publications as a freelancer; as a music journalist, Dylan probably did the same. I didn't mind sometimes making less than 30 cents a word; the heady thrill of the byline kept my young ego satisfied. And I was working full-time at a publication that had extremely flexible hours, allowing me to take on a magazine internship during the morning and work the main job until 8 or 9 pm.

As a young reporter, days are spent weaving through class as an outsider. You're there to report, to research, or critique. Public relations events were how I ate dinner some nights; even now as an almost 40-year-old woman, I haven't learned to tamp down the urge to devour all of the hors d'oeuvres at a cocktail party. The muscle memory of hungry nights stuck with me for a long time. Covering entertainment, as Dylan and I both did, gets you access that most people who aren't rich don't have, and certainly not access I was used to before I started working. Evenings were a blur of backstage passes, near front-row tickets, VIP nightclub sections, free drinks here, skip the line there.

It was the first that I'd seen how people lived who presumably had money or access. I'm sure I conflated the two. Sliding behind the scenes into these more affluent worlds—even through the smokescreen of the entertainment or nightlife scene—made me acutely aware of how different my life was by comparison, even with its various privileges. Freelance reporters in the 1990s through the early aughts could make anything between $10,000 per year (that the government knew about), to the six figures that the fabulist Stephen Glass made writing for *Rolling Stone*, *George* and *Harper*'s before his plagiarism at *The New Republic* was discovered.

Lethem wrote that Dylan had "slowly ground (myself) into $30,000 of credit card debt as a free-lancer," with most of his money coming from the work he did writing liner notes for a record label. The progressive or alt-weekly publications we worked for targeted social inequality in their reporting all the time, but the open secret was that unless one was employed there full time, you couldn't actually live on what they were paying. You worked there because you believed in the editorial missions, not because you believed that they had the ability to pay living wages.

The magazine job paid about $17,000 after taxes. My father had picked up second-shift janitorial jobs, cleaning planes at the airport and bathrooms at UWM. My mother was taking on extra jobs with Milwaukee Public Schools after-school programs in addition to her full-time teaching position. I could pretend to be upwardly mobile at parties but my regular life involved putting $4 (in quarters) worth of gas in my car sometimes and paying my cell phone bills two months behind schedule. Sherman Park was changing, largely due to the unemployment and deindustrialization that was gutting the region. Occasional gunshots in the neighborhood were a new thing. Burglaries were more frequent, and a drug house had set openly set up shop around the block where my sister and I used to walk to our Girl Scout meetings.

When I moved back to Milwaukee after college in 2001, the unemployment rate among people age 18-49 in the metro area was 28.1 percent compared with the national average of 34.1 percent. For white people in the Milwaukee metro area, the unemployment rate was 29.6 percent. For black working-age people, the unemployment rate was 44.9 percent.[5]

In my second year at the education magazine, which was located in the then-gentrifying east side Riverwest neighborhood, a poet friend from high school told me about a new apartment she had just moved into. She said the apartments, situated in an old furniture factory on the south side of town, had income guidelines to move in. "You can be broke but not poor," as she described it.

CHAPTER 3

PĄCZKIS TO ELOTES

In 1900, Albert P. Kunzelmann and his brother Joseph Esser opened the Kunzelmann & Esser furniture shop on 4th and Mitchell Street on Milwaukee's South Side.[6] Kunzelmann & Esser was located in a bustling retail district in the middle of a large Polish community; the Kunzelmann family had emigrated from Germany in the late 1800s. The store, which sold high-priced home goods, was so profitable that in 1909, the owners added an eight-story fireproof brick building to its retail holdings. By the 1970s, the neighborhood had changed significantly. The community had shifted from mostly Polish immigrants to Mexican nationals and first- and second-generation Mexican Americans. The high-end retail was starting to leave the area, though bridal shops and bakeries remained. Elotes replaced pączkis as the neighborhood snack, and the accordions had more norteño flavor than polka. Sunday Mass remained constant.

In 2001, a year after the furniture store closed, a Madison real estate developer purchased the historical building. The developer planned to renovate and turn it into affordable housing lofts for artists. They installed a gallery in the middle of the building and it became a stop on the city's Gallery Night for visual artists. They exposed the brick and refinished the original hardwood floors. There was a kiln in the basement and a darkroom for photographers. The renovation was being billed as the neighborhood's second coming, a sign that everything was going to be fancy again, really soon.

My entry-level editorial salary positioned me squarely into the mandated income bracket for tenants. And there, amidst a building full of working creatives, I freelanced stories for alternative weeklies and local magazines, I took long baths and smoked pot and fantasized about being rich or at least working for the *New York Times*. And I tried to figure out how to live as an adult, whatever that might have entailed.

But this little experiment on Mitchell, unlike the developer's market rate lofts in the Historic Fifth Ward less than a mile away, was slow to affect change. The same old-school bridal shops ringed the other side of the block. No restaurants were forthcoming (though this has changed considerably within the past 10 years); the bars catered to a much older clientele. There was no major grocery store within walking distance and the city's transit system suffered significant funding cuts so the routes were no longer as efficient. I was never a victim of crime, but I can remember during my regular walks through the neighborhood and seeing a man casually punch out windows on cars across the street, grabbing radios and anything else. Gang violence was also affecting families all over the neighborhood.

Living in the neighborhood. I liked it. But I was impatient, for a lot of things. Impatient for my then-boyfriend to decide that he loved me more than his own dreams (shitty, I know). Impatient for the neighborhood to look and be as cool as the Chicago neighborhoods I'd started slipping away to on the weekends. Impatient for my journalism career to blossom in the way that I had heard about in J-school. I only understood the forces of what was happening in the city from a relatively superficial place. I still yearned to leave Milwaukee eventually. The city wasn't where I felt like I could deal with my identity—whatever that was shaping up to be—in a way that felt satisfying for me.

In 2004, three things happened: I became one of the nearly 45 percent of working-age black people unemployed in the city when the education magazine laid me off. I was on soft money and the grant wasn't renewed.

The second thing that happened was that I applied for unemployment benefits and my grandmother offered to help me cover the portion of my rent that was still left over after applying the benefits and freelance money. It's the same kind of assistance I'm going to assume Dylan would have received from Abraham when times were really rough, especially if he had humbled himself enough to ask. Despite being surprisingly productive during unemployment, freelancing cover stories for alt-weeklies and magazines, by autumn my unemployment benefits were running out with no full-time journalism jobs materializing.

The third thing that happened was that I accidentally got pregnant.

The thing about getting pregnant, and what I decided to do after that are significant in terms of the story I thought I was telling. Because my relationship to gentrification, my origin story, isn't just rooted in my family planning choice. It also goes back to my grandmother.

My maternal grandparents chose to only have one child—my mother. This was largely because my grandmother, as the first college graduate among her siblings, wanted to work. Both of my grandparents worked good jobs and had only one child, so despite the segregation that shaped their other life choices, like housing or salary, they managed to create a reasonable amount of generational wealth. This translated into money that helped pay for my and my sisters' undergraduate education, and money that helped me with rent while I was freelancing. It translated into being a person with options, someone with privileges who more or less thrived even under systemic inequality. In this sense Dylan and I both could situate ourselves within the American lie of equal opportunity granted by hard work.

For several reasons, I made the decision with my partner at the time to have an abortion. As the eldest, I understood the investments that had been made on my behalf for my success and I felt pressure to conform to respectability standards. I assumed that moving ahead with an unplanned, out-of-wedlock pregnancy would have meant a complete cut off of financial support and a swift end to the journalism career I'd been working so hard for. I also wanted to be on stronger financial and professional footing before I started a family.

Less than two months after the abortion, I packed up my meager belongings, including my copy of *The Fortress of Solitude*, and moved to Chicago to look for work. I moved into my grandmother's house in Chatham. She fed me and gave me money to make copies of my resume at Kinko's and get my hair done for job interviews. She put up with my obnoxious quarter-life crisis complaining. She never judged me for heading out to the clubs to dance to house music on Saturday nights and she never allowed me to make her late for church on Sunday morning. Even though it was at times stressful, in hindsight, it was one of the places I look back in life as where I felt the most authentic.

On the South Side I *belonged* somewhere. I would see aunts, uncles, cousins on the 87 bus, and sometimes older women in the neighborhood confused me for my mom. I loved it. I had history. Context. Something rooting me in an authentic place that I was actually happy about, unlike Dylan, on the run just like his mother Rachel/Running Crab. When I was working, I took the Red Line "L" train in the morning and the Number 3 bus on King Drive back home every night. My speech, formerly clipped and vowel-stingy like most Sconnies, became a looser, up-south interpretation reflecting the mouths of elders with Mississippi roots. I had found a part-time job at the historic *Chicago Defender*, and I was blasting the new Common album *Be* out of my car windows like everyone else. In Chatham, I wasn't an outsider anymore. I found what Dylan seemingly couldn't.

I saved money from two part-time editorial jobs and eventually moved to Hyde Park for a couple of years where the residents had for decades been locked in bitter battles with the University of Chicago[7] over property creep and racial restriction covenants. Residents were also deeply suspicious of development, in an attempt to stave off the hypergentrification moving like The Blob through certain north side neighborhoods. The lack of new development gave the neighborhood a low-key, folksy vibe. The small businesses, bookstores and cafes had been there forever, giving Hyde Park a continuity that was nice, even if it occasionally felt like living under a bubble.

I deeply loved living near all of my friends, going to Valois for breakfast in the summers, lingering at the Hyde Park Arts Festival, or eating Italian Fiesta and drinking booze while doing our laundry, but due to the segregation defining borders in all 77 of Chicago's neighborhoods, I did not enjoy always having to trek to the north side to go dancing on a Friday or Saturday night, or go see concerts, or film festivals or drive more than a few miles to get to reasonably priced grocery stores (the Hyde Park co-op was a bit pricey for me). Much of my social life was spent at various locations up north. And why not? I was in my 20s, Funky Buddha Lounge in West Town was still one of the best places to be in the city. But pre-Uber or Lyft, cab drivers weren't trying to take people back out south if, God forbid, you wanted to be responsible and not drink and drive.

Gentrification was changing Chicago in other neighborhoods to an extreme degree. I saw how northwest side neighborhoods like Wicker Park and Bucktown shifted from working-class white and Latinx to affluent whites. My white friends who were not-rich members of the creative class were priced out, and they started moving farther and farther west through the neighborhoods, past Western Avenue or to Logan Square, which was in the earliest of gentrification stages back then. My black friends generally clustered in the South Loop, Woodlawn, Chatham, Bronzeville, South Shore, and Hyde Park.

During that time, I worked for the *The Chicago Reporter*, an award-winning magazine that focused on issues of race and poverty. *TCR* documented the six and seven-figure flipping of Near North Side real estate that started once the City of Chicago announced that the Cabrini-Green public housing projects would be torn down over a period of time. Cabrini-Green was sitting on prime real estate: less than a mile from downtown and Lake Michigan, including North Avenue Beach and the Magnificent Mile; it sat right off of the Kennedy Expressway; and it was between several main cross streets for easy movement around the city. Several years went by between the demolition announcement in 1999 and when the towers actually came down in 2011, but flips started in anticipation, in some cases, less than 24 hours after the announcement.[8] In contrast, the gentrification of Gowanus took more than half of Dylan's life. Isabel Vendle never lived to see it. Lethem describes those who remained, like Lala or Arthur Lomb, like survivors of a war—weary and dazed. And they are survivors of what was at that point a 20-year escalation of police brutality, drugs, disinvestment and mass incarceration.

In the late 1990s and early aughts, Cabrini was the latest example of a mass removal of African Americans from public housing throughout the city, breaking up generations of families and interpersonal support systems. People were promised that they would have the opportunity to move into either nearby public housing buildings or other Section 8 units across the city. By the time I moved to town, it was clear that had always been a false promise and the only goal had been removal of the tenants, with little concern as to where or how they would land. Waitlists for any new housing were years-long and full of restrictions that turned off former residents, such as no loud music or outside barbecues, or rules that made them ineligible, such as being related to people who had been convicted of crimes.

By the time I moved to the Near North Side in 2008, gentrification was in full swing. A newish Dominick's grocery store had been built, and some of the Cabrini-Green towers had already been evacuated and demolished. Wells Street between LaSalle Boulevard and North Avenue was filling with boutiques, restaurants and lounges. I lived above a Domino's Pizza on the corner of LaSalle and Division Avenue—a symbolic vantage point from which to view the changes. Gold Coast to my right, the Cabrini-Green towers to my left, Planned Parenthood on one corner, the Mark Twain Hotel rooming house on the other corner, still frequented by extremely vulnerable populations such as sex workers and people struggling with drug addiction.[9]

I was working full time, with a freelance gig or two in my back pocket. I attended a lot of elite events happening in the city around that same time, by the way of the access that journalism and friends in the service industry provided, but I wasn't opening those doors on my own. I'd go places and pretend I belonged. Study the mannerisms, make mental notes of the things people would reference that I hadn't been aware of and hope that my clothes weren't too faded or tight to reveal me as a broke imposter. I would walk home from work some nights and smell steak cooking at the Zagat-rated restaurants in the Rush Street area, wondering what it was like to be able to afford to eat there without having to look at my bank account afterwards. Wondered if I'd ever be able to just work one job and have the salary cover everything, if I'd ever be able to afford a home. That may have been a critical difference between Dylan and I; his aesthestic snobbery shunned middle-class aspirations.

Not only does Dylan not seem to have an interest in having a home or family, he runs far away from what he does have. I didn't want to run, but the economic state of the country, especially during the Great Recession, left me feeling trapped in Chicago. My salary wasn't moving, my publisher was folding magazines and cutting staff on the business side. A relationship—if I could be loose enough with language to categorize it that way—I was in at the time wasn't really going anywhere either. It was the first time that I started thinking about leaving—both Chicago and the journalism career that I'd worked so hard to get a toehold in. Watching the ageism my dad experienced after his layoff, coupled with the stories of journalists who were getting laid off after 20 years, made me think that I needed a Plan B, just in case.

Living in that in-between place, at a very in-between point of my life, I started to really understand about the systemic issues that were hard to escape, and the way that segregation, poverty, education, and healthcare interacted to affect lives that were already behind the starting line. The limitations of my own privilege were coming into focus as a black woman who wasn't behind the starting line, but who didn't come from the kind of wealth to insulate me from economic anxiety. The Near North Side exposed to me the full extremes between Oprah rich and homelessness. I came home many nights confused, angry and uncomfortable about what I seeing play out in the streets, but felt hopeless about the situation and kept it to myself. The lie was revealing itself. Things had never been fair.

CHAPTER 4

GOOD ENOUGH

I Have Met the Enemy—And it is Me!
(Superman #329)

Dylan only really moved one time, though a cross country is so major, he could be forgiven for not wanting to move again. I moved to Lexington, Kentucky, in 2012 to be with my then-boyfriend, Delano. He had a job and a four-year-old daughter from a previous marriage and I reasoned that I could be a librarian anywhere. Lexington is ironically where Rachel Ebdus found herself for a man she loved, too, joining a commune and managing to get arrested there after she left Abraham and Dylan.

Lexington is a city in a state with a host of contradictions and idiosyncrasies. It's a former slave-holding Union state. Lexington is a blue city surrounded by an ocean of Bible Belt red. It's also a place of extreme wealth—driven by the horse industry, which contributed $3.5 billion to the state's overall economy in 2011—that co-exists alongside extreme poverty.[10] Given these contradictions, it's little wonder that Lexington was the place that I became a black gentrifier. It's where Dylan's and my lived experiences diverge, where race, class, and gender transform someone into a hero or enemy in the eyes of neighbors, and where I had to start making choices about how and where to live as a reflection of my values, versus Dylan, who through his privilege is allowed to passively move through life with assumptions that only serve to benefit or positively affirm his choices.

Lexington's urban boundary is a traditional model of a core business district downtown and everything else radiates from that nucleus until it hits what Lexington-Fayette County calls the Urban Service Boundary and transitions into the rural part of the county. Lexington, which was in 2017 named one of the third-least diverse cities in the United States, is also highly segregated.[11] The majority of African Americans in the city live in the East End/Martin Luther King/Broadway Avenue neighborhoods adjacent to the downtown area. The city was so segregated that a historic hand-drawn map of the city from the mid-20th century shows a former public housing project separated into a "Whites Only" tower and a "Colored" tower. Segregated, even in poverty.

Before I moved to town, Delano was living beyond the edge of the urban service boundary. City girl that I am, I asked him if we could move into an apartment in the more densely populated downtown area. I knew there would be more people who looked like us in that community, and the Martin Luther King neighborhood was perfectly situated between three main libraries that I was targeting for employment. It wasn't so much that I knew anything about the neighborhood per se, but after apartment hunting in larger cities, I knew how to intepret the Craigslist dog whistles of "original hardwood floors" and "downtown urban living."

We found a first-floor apartment in a lime-green duplex on a one-block strip called Johnson Avenue, formerly Johnson Highway, that was right next to a nice-sized city park. His daughter had been accepted to a public school that was less than a 10-minute drive from the apartment, and we were in walking distance of downtown and the aforementioned libraries. The average salary for the neighborhood was $19,450 and at the time, 50.1 percent of the residents lived in poverty, according to the 2010 Census. So, in essence, the MLK neighborhood was not that different from the neighborhoods I had been living in as a young, single journalist.

The landlord was a near-elderly white woman who made daily drives up and down the block in her white minivan. She would tend to the garden in front of our apartment and walk her labradoodle around. We regarded her as relatively innocuous, but within the first few months living there, we learned the truth: Over several years, she had purchased much of the block we were living on, flipped the houses and sold or rented them to youngish couples or individuals like ourselves. She marked her flips by painting the brick houses, lemon here, paisley there. Her resources created a pace of flipping houses—mostly bought with cash during sheriff's department auctions—that was more machine-like than any of Vendle's machinations. Her actions created considerable controversy throughout the downtown neighborhoods; people we knew who had purchased homes from her alleged that the renovations had been done sloppily. They bought the homes at a markup and then had to go back and spend a lot of money on critical infrastructure projects, like sewage lines or roofs. The apartment we had chosen, so cute in the Craigslist ads, had a major rodent issue and mold in the bathroom.

We realized that we had been "vetted" for approval when the landlord began dropping hints to us about houses around the corner that she was rehabbing and selling. She wanted to know if we were interested. "What does it mean that she finds us 'good enough'?" I asked Delano one afternoon. There was no one else in the neighborhood who looked like us moving in. There were still some older black families or empty nesters on our block, but no younger black families to comple-ment the remaining families or replace the ones who had already left.

A quiet, well-manicured house stood in the middle of Johnson Avenue. During the neighborhood holiday potluck, we found out through casual conversation that the elderly black woman who had been living there died more than a year earlier and the house was just sitting vacant. Waiting. "That one," Delano would say, pointing to it during our neighborhood walks. "You have to have the vision." The only vision I could see was all the work we'd have to do. The front steps had green astroturf. The backyard had a carport made up of concrete a couple feet deep. I wasn't convinced.

But he wasn't convinced that we should overspend on one of our landlord's flipped houses on the other side of the park, where his daughter would have less proximity to the neighborhood kids, who were prone to running barefoot from yard to yard on hot summer days or building snow forts together in the winter. We had also made friends with some of the other neighbors on our block. Summer barbecues, cocktails on the porch, helping each other with gardens or meal rotations for new parents was a daily part of our life there. I had joined the neighborhood association and Delano could bike to his job. We knew we wanted to stay on Johnson but buying a turn-key property was out of our price range. Not to mention Lexington's downtown housing stock is disproportionately made up of shotgun houses—nothing you could raise a growing family in—or mansions that non-horse-owning millionaires can't afford.

We wrote a letter to the woman's son in the spring, inquiring about the property. We didn't ask outright about a sale and we were prepared to hear a no, but we had also done our homework. We talked about gentrification and mentioned that we were a black couple looking to settle down and expand our family. Two months later, in the late spring of 2013, and after an unexpected gift from my in-laws, we became the latest owners of the house. The owner sold the home to directly to us, with no realtor. He said our letter had come at the exact time he felt ready to sell, especially since he lived out west and had no plans to move back to Kentucky. We also found out later that a couple of the older black residents on the block with whom the son had grown up placed a call to him on our behalf to persuade him to sell to us. As he and his wife prepped the house for sale, he gifted me with a small collection of some of his mother's recipes—she had been known to throw regular parties for neighbors and other people in the MLK/East End communities. Her elegant marginalia curled in the edges of the notecards detailing for whom she had cooked certain things and whether or not the recipe was liked or if she had made any substitutions. She had loved living on Johnson Avenue. "I think she would be really happy that you two are moving into the house," her son told us. "She knew how this neighborhood was changing."

The home had been built in 1910, and the elderly woman had only been its third occupant. We had to gut everything down to the studs and brick. Whole walls came down; the house was a skeleton, stripped to its essence: a frame, a roof, doorways. My husband and

I, like many of the white families who had purchased a home on the block, saved some money by swinging sledgehammers ourselves against the plaster walls for a few weeks. We pulled an entire fireplace apart brick by brick from the roof to the crawlspace and pulled up all of the carpets so the contractor could expose the original pine floors.

We lived below our means and had a manageable mortgage. Our combined incomes were significantly higher than the neighborhood average, and we knew we could absorb any property tax increases. As the months went by, we watched the property value assessor's website with interest and shock. Had we become the *gentry*? And if not the gentry, the boho cultural class, like Rachel and Abraham? We could clearly see where our purchase of the home had increased housing values significantly for the entire block and was affecting sales across the neighborhood. That's how it works, really. But I felt uncomfortable knowing that we were responsible for property tax increases that our other black neighbors would have to absorb, the neighbors who advocated on our behalf.

Even though our house was painted fire-engine red on the outside, we understood that our position in the neighborhood was very gray. We were outsiders,

Yankees whose ability to purchase a home via an intergenerational wealth transfer and fix it up with bank assistance was potentially putting vulnerable neighbors at risk. It was like stepping into Bizarro World. We all thought we were the good guys, but maybe we weren't after all.

The wealth transfer is the whispered about thing, dropped casually over drinks or a slip of the tongue. A relative died and left money that went toward a new roof, private school tuition, or paying a contractor to renovate bathrooms. A grandparent wrote a check for childcare or a new vehicle. One of the things that keeps class differences entrenched, like unequal pay in the workplace, is the fact that social rules say it's not polite to discuss money outright, no doubt to quell anger when the true inequalities are revealed. It builds on the myth of the rugged individualism of the "American Dream." I did it by myself. No help. Bootstraps high as fuck.

Disclosures about wealth transfer are generally made with an apologetic smile or revealed so quickly you'd miss that tidbit if you weren't paying attention. But it stands to reason that some of us are getting some kind of financial assistance, as national average wages have stagnated over the past 30 years, and even more so in the 16 years that I've been working since getting my bachelor's degree. Our block was made up of pink-collar, creative class workers. We had archivists, social workers, museum curators, professors, photographers, chefs, poets, service industry workers, and nonprofit employees—not people known to be paid like, say, Fortune 500 CEOs.

To suggest that *everyone* is making homeownership happen without any intergenerational assistance whatsoever is to perpetuate an even bigger lie than the ones that we already tell ourselves about our true role in gentrifying spaces. Urban areas are full of creative class or "knowledge economy" workers whose families are subsidizing some aspect of living, where the rent totals far beyond what most of those workers make in a year. Where my husband and I were different is that we had family members who managed to save enough money to pass some on to their children in the way that white families generally do. Dylan might not have personally exemplified this statistic, but a 2014 study by the Institute for Women's Policy and Research revealed that a single white male has 160 times the wealth of a single woman of color.[12] My maternal grandmother helped pay for my college education, but my grandparents only had one child and they both worked jobs that paid well at a time when it was possible to run a household on one income.

The Ebdus family falls into that category of people who may have access to intergenerational wealth. They can afford to pay a contractor to help renovate the home, but they also take in renters in the smaller apartment. Rachel has a part-time job at the phone company, but that's not the kind of job that turns people into the one percent. In discussions of money, Rachel blithely suggests that it's not an issue to access money for Dylan to go to private school.

Dylan, kept by his parents at arm's length from discussions of money and privilege, moves through his life purposefully ignorant. He lapses into debt pursuing his journalism career but has family who would send him money if he needed it. More than that, he seems to have a general apathy about money. It's clear to him in college that he's not affluent, but he doesn't appear to be unduly stressed out about it as he gets older. Dylan isn't interested in the kinds of major lifestyle decisions that require a lot of money, like buying a house or having a family.

Like the Ebdus family, my family statistically overlaps into a lot of categories of people who prefer to live in urban areas. In *Mobilities and Inequality*, European sociologists created an empirical study focused on the city of Cologne, Germany, showing that gender, education, ethnicity and family size weigh heavily in who chooses to live in urban areas.[13] "Respondents with a university degree are more likely to live in an inner-city neighbourhoods than others and the same is true for immigrants and women." Academics are more likely to choose inner-city neighborhoods as are, curiously, people who identified as enjoying suspense or thrills in their life.[14]

The study even pointed to leisure preferences as reasons for living in urban neighborhoods. As someone who grew up with exposure to the arts and then picked a cultural heritage-based career, I enjoy living near cultural institutions. I loved being in walking distance to the Siskel Theater in Chicago so I could see film festivals with friends, being able to take a 15-minute train ride to Downtown Crossing in Boston and see a concert, or living near libraries and bookstores so I could take in free book readings by various authors.

The American Bourgeoisie: Distinction and Identity in the Nineteenth Century lays plain the unoriginality regarding leisure preferences and retail that tends to shape gentrifying neighborhoods. "The Steady Supporters of Order: American Mechanics' Institute Fairs as Icons of

Bourgeois Culture" draws a distinct parallel between the institute fairs of the 1800s and the makerspaces, night markets, and fleas of today's gentrified areas. "These manufacturers…became patrons of the arts by insisting on the parallel between national economic improvement and aesthetic innovation, between manufacturing and art making." The book also points to interior design and food as being of part of the gentry's conspicuous consumption.

In *The Fortress of Solitude*, Dylan's third-person narrator points to restaurants as a sign of the coming gentry. "Some eager beaver's opened a French restaurant on Bergen and Hoyt, jumping the gun perhaps but worth a shot." While many years later, Arthur Lomb takes up where Isabel Vendle left off, owning several buildings on Smith Street, including a small bistro.

I couldn't extricate my history from the food, either. There was nothing like visiting Lexington's downtown farmer's market for the first time and reading the historical marker near the courthouse that revealed the space as a former slave auction site. I looked around, seeing people casually purchase heirloom tomatoes in the same place where a child was ripped from her mother, where a man's flesh was seared with hot irons as a receipt of sale. I had never experienced the farmer's market in that context before, having only lived in non-slave-owning states. It was hard for me to reconcile that contrast; I started my own backyard garden shortly after we moved into our new home.

Food in gentrified spaces is also about erasure, a fact amplified in the summer of 2017, when some burgeoning Portland, Oregon, taco truck owners were criticized for saying that they harassed native Mexican women for their authentic tortilla recipes only to turn around and sell the tacos for what was undoubtedly a higher price point. That's to say nothing of the exceptionally obnoxious habit of restaurant owners in gentrified neighborhoods using negative stereotypes of the inner city or AAVE slang as a theme or item name: Pho Sho in Atlanta, the restaurant in Crown Heights that sold 40-ounce bottles of malt liquor in an actual brown paper bag, or "Doughp" (pronounced "dope"), a San Francisco pop-up store selling cookie dough mixes with names like "The OG" and "This S'More is Hella Lit."[15]

Alongside the empirical study, a 2009 National Institutes of Health study showed that affluent African Americans end up living in segregated, low-income areas more often than affluent white people, resulting from a mix of preference and systemic segregation that allowed few other options.[16] The *New York Times* profiled some Milwaukee couples in a piece about middle-class families moving back to all-black, but poorer neighborhoods after experiencing racism and microaggressions in the inner-ring suburbs. "It felt like that's where we should be," one of the women interviewed said about the urban areas.[17]

I am black and college-educated. I'm a woman between the ages of 18–39. I work in academia. According to the empirical study, those things mean that I'm more likely to live in an urban area. But it doesn't mean that other people who can't or aren't doing those things don't belong in the neighborhood as well. The study's authors were careful to point out in their conclusions and policy recommendations that "the fair distribution of both quality of life and access to mobility might become an undisputed aim of any urban policy that claims to be sustainable and integrated."

One aspect of city living currently drawing people back is the turn-of-the-century architecture and legacy buildings created public social spaces by billionaires like the Carnegie and Rockefeller families during America's Gilded Age. Heavily ornate Gothic-Revival architecture featured in public libraries, city halls, civic centers, and transit hubs that have been around since the 1800s provide what preservationist Tom Mayes calls a "continuity" of location for people to coalesce around. In a *Preservation Leadership Forum* blog, sponsored by the National Trust for Historic Preservation, Mayes said: "[I]n a world that is constantly changing, old places provide people with a sense of being part of a continuum that is necessary for them to be psychologically and emotionally healthy."

However, the buildings tend to amplify the mythology of and nostalgia for pioneers and settlers. Seldom does historic preservation engage with the full truth: that historical buildings need millions of dollars for infill projects because they were allowed to lapse into disrepair when white flight emptied the cities of the white people for whom those structures were originally built.

People use the historical buildings as a proxy for their values. Valuing a brick home or pursuing infill projects isn't just about age or design, it's also about labor. It's a shorthand for a time when people made their living with their hands and they were skilled at it. Architecture tells stories too, of merchant or intelligentsia classes who forced slaves or hired immigrant white laborers to build their homes—imposing buildings with turrets and gables or other aristocratic European architectural signifiers, fortified with wrought iron, and hiding secret entrances or doors for servants who were supposed to be invisible.

Ironically, even if the buildings are unique, gentrification breeds uniformity. Certain touches become ubiquitous: address numbers with the "Shake Shack" minimalist font, lines as smooth and clean as any Apple product; interior design touches like Edison bulbs, apron-front sinks, and wooden slat privacy fences. The latest designs are heavy on nostalgia for a pre-Industrial Era past; the woodwork and the farmhouse details intimate an "artisanal" touch that circles back to the makerspace ethos in *The American Bourgeosie*.

When I lived in Lexington, I was interested in the idea of historic preservation as a reflection of our intertwined histories, from the raw materials to a building or neighborhood's actual history. For instance, were really excited to be able to work with a black bricklayer who had been running his business for more than 30 years. He and his crew expertly tended to and tuck-pointed our brick fireplace, which had almost been destroyed by a separate subcontractor. The bricklayers were so happy to see a black family moving into the home that they even added an additional step for us onto the front of the house to make it easier on our older relatives' knees when visiting.

Professionally, I wrote a National Register of Historic Places application on behalf of a community development organization for a former Greyhound bus terminal in the North Limestone neighborhood, at the very edge of downtown. The application, which was accepted in 2013, was part of a larger plan to turn the building into an indoor market for local small merchants, including people of color, in the neighborhood. The project later received a Knight Foundation planning grant, although the building has not yet been developed.[18]

I became so interested in the idea of building preservation that I applied and was accepted to a graduate certificate program in historic preservation at the University of Kentucky in 2017. My interest dovetailed with an archival collection of architectural blueprints from an influential Lexington firm that my students were processing that year. The students used the collection as a starting point to research various aspects of the built environment; one design student had an interest in public transit and found a relationship between racial covenants in Lexington's downtown neighborhoods and the development of transit routes. His work confirmed my hypothesis, which was that transit funding and routes were stunted in the areas near downtown where there were more African Americans, and it was more robust in areas that were white. But guiding him toward the archival documents at the city's Planning Department to discover the fact on his own affirmed what I think is most compelling about using history to reveal inequality and advocate for change.

When it comes to creating a home, how does one reconcile individual needs with the greater community impact? What do we love and why? Are they choices, or does everything merely radiate out from structural inequality? Dylan had no say in his parents moving to Gowanus, but he likely made residential location decisions as an adult based on his perceived safety or ease of living as a white male, just like I made decisions based on things that I prioritized as a black woman, a professional who had no car, and a young person with an active social life. But nothing ever happens in a vacuum.

In trying to create communities built on the lie of nostalgia, it's understood that there were always people for whom this idealized vision of community was never fully realized. That the black middle-class enclaves created on the South Side of Chicago were built on the foundation of segregation, of racism and restricted movements, even if we could use public bathrooms. That the decisions my husband and I made about housing were directly connected to our individual experiences with segregation, growing up in both suburban and urban spaces, respectively, and that the experiences of our parents and grandparents were a result of or reaction to that same segregation. It's understanding that the origin story of gentrification and the communities we've built or destroyed purposely through policy were designed for exclusion. Even though Dylan and I had similar experiences in our youth and the cities in which we lived, privilege and identities place us on opposite sides of the lie, even though I think we both see through it.

PART II
BIG BADS

———

The Price of Progress
(DC Comics Presents #54)

As Dylan traversed between his worlds, there were ultimately things he had to confront or experience to move forward to the next stage of his life. In the comic books he and Mingus fervently consume those experiences could more accurately be represented by a supervillain—frequently called "Big Bads." Dylan bore most of his bullying with a mixture of annoyance and resignation, but a yoking by Dean Street bully Robert Woolfolk was akin to a Superman showdown with General Zod. In navigating the many struggles of gentrification, three major things stand out as Big Bads that must be reckoned with—issues that affect gentrification as much as gentrification is affected by them and they feed on each other in a cyclical way: education, policing, and housing policies. This is a trilogy so powerful you'd need the whole Justice League and the Avengers together to try and fight it. Each of those elements are extremely potent on their own but together they interact to solidify existing systems of oppression and create alternate realities for different people, even those living right next door to each other.

CHAPTER 5

PHANTOM ZONE

Education is an early and consistent narrative thread driving different plots in *The Fortress of Solitude*. It starts with Rachel's very intentional decision to send Dylan to public school, where, she bragged that "He's one of three white children in the whole school. Not his class, not his grade—the whole school," to his admittance to citywide magnet school Stuyvesant High, which marked his escape from Brooklyn, to his acceptance to Camden College. Camden is where Dylan's lies of omission become fully-realized falsehoods. Dylan is never above lying to fit in, but his attempts at embodying an "authentic Brooklyn" persona make a grotesque mockery of his real friendship with Mingus. It's not the first time he sold out his friend to try and fit in. In a way, Dylan's actions embody the series of lies that America was built on: not just the lies of betrayal, erasure and theft, but the lie of pretending that none of those things are meaningful to the present.

Education affects the lives of Dylan's Dean Street cohort; entire life trajectories rose or fell based on middle or high school acceptance letters. In the March 26, 2017, issue of *The New Yorker* magazine, Lethem was interviewed for a profile about his childhood friend, Pulitzer-winning playwright Lynn Nottage, who also grew up on Dean Street. Lethem recalled a conversation in which he quoted Nottage as saying that everyone from the Dean Street neighborhood they knew either "went into jail or law enforcement," and that education was a huge factor. Nottage and Lethem attended The High School for Music & Art in Manhattan and graduated in 1982, commuting every day across class and racial lines. Lethem said he specifically modeled the character of Henry after Nottage's brother, who currently works as an assistant district attorney in New York.

Education can either create more of a divide or equalize a playing field. The system creates insiders and outsiders, people who can move in or alongside mainstream society, and those who find themselves completely shut out of it. Just as my life was shaped by the presence of segregation, it was similarly shaped by the educational choices that were made for me throughout my life.

My mom was a public school teacher who knew how the system worked. I was a product of magnet program public schools and tracking. When I couldn't win a citywide lottery for one of the main Milwaukee Public Schools' magnet high schools, my parents—and largely at the urging of my Catholic father—sent me to a mostly-white Catholic high school, though my two younger sisters won their individual lotteries and attended two separate magnet public schools that were geared toward college prep.

Twentieth century white flight wasn't just about real estate property values; it was also about public schools and federally-ordered desegregation. The iconic photograph of a white Boston resident attempting to impale an African American with the sharp end of the American flag over a busing and desegregation program epitomizes the violence that greeted desegregation and the lengths that some white people were willing to go to avoid it—from the 1954 Supreme Court ruling on Brown vs. the Topeka, Kansas, Board of Education that ruled separate but equal schools unconstitutional all the way through the 21st century, where people are pushing to create their own townships to resegregate their schools. Moving away to the suburbs was one option for those seeking to avoid desegregation. Creating specialty programs within public schools that catered to white parents was another option. White people sought out private or religious schools, ones that had no mandate to accept black or brown kids; that could accept any student as long as their parents were paying tuition; cherry-pick children who performed exceptionally well on entrance exams; and reject without consequence poor children, children with special needs, or children of any race who had significant social needs.

Moving to the suburbs for families of color was not always an option, as there were and are still locations with had race-based covenants and communities that are extremely hostile to black or brown families. Just because suburban districts could be desegregated didn't mean they were welcoming spaces. In the 1980s, I had an extremely brief stint in Milwaukee's so-named "Chapter 220" integration program, which began busing Milwaukee kids to suburban school districts in 1976. That ended after a racist stunt in which the bus driver purposely dropped me, a four-year-old, off in front of my house alone instead of the babysitter's house, which was the prearranged stop. A kind neighbor saw me and brought me inside of her house. Gave me Kool-Aid and kept an eye on the window, waiting for my mom to return home. My parents weren't even really acquainted with this neighbor, but she saw me outside unaccompanied and knew there was a problem.

Friends of mine who attended all-white schools when they were a bit older, especially black women, experienced social isolation around dating, as did I at an all-white Catholic high school. As a black girl, no one is asking you to prom unless you can procure a date from a public school or maybe on the low you end up attending with a cousin or family friend (as I did also). I remember having classmates who would openly talk about how prejudiced their family members were. And for the tiny number of white guys with whom there was a clear mutual crush, I knew there would never, ever be any impetus to act on it. Imagine experiencing unilateral rejection at a time when desire for physical acceptance is so keen.

As it happened, my first editorial job was at a national education magazine based on the east side of Milwaukee that was part-pedagogical guide, part-public school advocacy and activism and fundamentally against charter schools. Milwaukee was ground zero for the charter school movement, which deeply divided parents and educators about the implications for black children left behind in schools where the gap between the extremely poor and the extremely affluent was growing from a gap to a canyon. People of color who had resources began leaving urban public schools as well, following paths of flight to suburban school districts or moving their children into private, religious or charter schools. Black or brown children whose parents who didn't have resources were left behind in schools that had more students with needs than were resources to serve them. Surely many of those parents would have wanted to advocate for their kids the same way more affluent parents do, but those who work low-income or service economy jobs don't have the type of flexibility that allows parents to participate in parent-teacher associations or school fundraising efforts, and even if they could, there's not much money they would be able to raise to obtain the types of supplemental enrichment programs that more well-resourced schools offer.

Gentrifiers who have children and insist on keeping them out of public schools further entrench poor-performing neighborhood schools in the margins, along with any of the social problems that accompany them.

And even gentrifiers who don't have children should be aware of this point. I'd go to the neighborhood block club meetings in Lexington and hear the hipsters complain about robberies or panhandlers and wonder how they didn't see the connection between the lack of good schools or jobs in our neighborhood and an increase in robberies or drug dealing.

New York Times Magazine writer Nikole Hannah-Jones, who has written extensively about public schools and resegregation, penned a 2016 article for the magazine about choosing an elementary school for her daughter that altered the texture of the conversations my husband and I were having about schooling our children.[19] Hannah-Jones discussed the irony of and tension between writing about school and housing segregation while living in a gentrifying neighborhood and feeling ambivalent about choosing a neighborhood public school. After a series of fraught conversations, she and her husband decided to send their daughter to the neighborhood public school instead of a specialty magnet or private school. The children at her daughter's school are mostly black or Latinx, and at least half had incomes low enough to qualify for the free lunch program, but Hannah-Jones said her previous work convinced her that "saying my child deserved access to 'good' public schools felt like implying that children in 'bad' schools deserved the schools they got, too."

The discussions she and her husband had marked a sharp contrast to Rachel Ebdus' rationale for sending Dylan to a public school; Rachel seemed to feel, somewhat condescendingly, that Dylan could teach things to black children at school. "It's a problem for him to solve, school. I did it, so can he," she told Isabel Vendle. Rachel's relative privilege meant that she could make that decision without worrying that it would drastically alter the trajectory of Dylan's life, in which infinite possibilities would still unfurl before him. Hannah-Jones' husband wondered if she "was asking him to expose our child to the type of education that the two of us had managed to avoid.… Hadn't we worked hard, he asked, frustration building in his voice, precisely so that she would not have to go to the types of schools that trapped so many black children?"

Hannah-Jones and her husband live in the rapidly gentrifying Brooklyn neighborhood of Bedford-Stuyvesant. Given their current professions and economic status, they decided that as a middle-class family, their presence could help them advocate for *all* of the kids at the school, and they felt confident in their ability to fill in whatever curricular or enrichment gaps were lacking. They spurned the idea of upholding the same systems of inequality that leave black and brown students behind.

Education's influence on gentrification doesn't stop at how it affects young children. Higher education plays a unique role in the gentrification ecosystem in urban areas, where universities push and pull on the surrounding communities to get what they want. In *The University and Urban Revival*, author Judith Rodin, describing changes the University of Pennsylvania took to change its relationship to the West Philadelphia community where campus is based, admitted that "for decades these institutions have flexed their huge muscles of property ownership and pushed their way into the surrounding area…as disgruntled homeowners were displaced to make room for the expansion of these institutions with newly available federal urban-renewal dollars."

Most cities I've lived in have urban-based universities that have had tumultuous historical relationships with their local communities. In 1949, the University of Kentucky in Lexington demolished the historically black Adamstown neighborhood near campus to build an athletic stadium.[20] And the University of Chicago is still remembered for its hostile stance toward the community—encouraging block clubs to discriminate against people from the surrounding and all-black Kenwood, Woodlawn and Englewood neighborhoods who would have wanted to live in Hyde Park, and pushing people out of those neighborhoods through major land acquisition through the 20th century.

Boston's real estate prices have long been astronomical and its myriad universities play a role—not *just* in terms of campus real estate creep but also the overwhelming numbers of students who come to pursue their higher education year after year, exploited by slumlords and left unprotected by inconsistent code enforcement. *The Boston Globe* ran a heartbreaking story in 2014 about a Boston University undergraduate in the Allston area who died in a house fire, largely because she was living in a building that had been illegally chopped up to fit too many people.[21] The student couldn't safely exit the building, and worse, the way the house had been subdivided acted as an accelerant for the fire, shooting flames directly up through the middle of the building.

My entire reason for moving to Boston placed me squarely within this context. I was part of the problem because I had little choice. When I moved there to attend graduate school at Simmons College in 2010, I was shocked to find out that the city was so expensive that I couldn't afford to live on my own as I had for the past several years. I found a place in the Roxbury neighborhood of Fort Hill that only had one room-mate and felt fortunate; most people I knew in Boston had a minimum of three other roommates. It fit the same criteria I'd been in for most of my adult life. Mostly black and brown neighborhood. Some housing projects. Some property crime but nothing that made me feel unsafe. The three-flat was a close walk to mass transit and walking distance to the school.

But the apartment itself had issues that I'd never experienced in Chicago. Our landlord, while some-what responsive, did little about the mice infestation in the building. In addition to eating rice in the cupboards, they ate holes in my underwear. Nothing is more harrowing than finding bite marks on one of your vibrators. The apartment was also poorly insu-lated, so much so that when I moved in in January, I could see my breath puffing out from underneath my three comforters when I woke up in the mornings. What worried me the most, however, was a door in my bedroom that presumably led to a balcony or fire escape. When I was actually able to jiggle the door open one day—as it was practically jammed shut—I discovered to my horror that there was nothing on the outside. Just the ground two stories below, with a gnarly tree that I likely would have broken my leg or back on had I passed it jumping to the ground in the event of a fire. But with Boston's extremely competitive rental market, I felt pressure to take the apartment the minute I saw it. Fort Hill was gentrifying when I moved in and that only increased in the years since I moved away.

Former city councilman Chuck Turner, who has been organizing around housing justice in Boston since the 1980s with the Greater Roxbury Neighborhood Association and other groups, is a current resident of Fort Hill; the home he and his wife own is only about a 10-minute walk from my former mousetrap. Fifty years ago, "Boston *was* a very affordable city," he told me. "It was a working man's city, from my perspective.… Today it's reached a point of financial extremity."

Turner said he and his wife bought their house in 1971 for $7,000. In 2017, homes on his block were selling for more than half a million dollars. Land control was a huge civil rights issue in Boston in the latter half of the 20th century, with the city buying lots of property and refusing to develop it. Turner and others have worked over the years through various initiatives: rent control, mediation process for land-lords prior to evictions, even purchasing homes through various housing justice organizations to use as a base for their activism. All of those things, and the more physical means of protesting unfair or illegal housing, such as putting one's body between an evicting sheriff and the house they are clearing out, are nothing, Turner said, without good paying jobs.

He pointed to a 2017 effort to get neighborhood construction workers hired on a project in nearby Dudley Square at $18 per hour—higher than the local minimum wage of $11 per hour. "It's seen as a win, but reality is $18 an hour means you're earning $36,000 a year. So it's an improvement but individually, it's not. It's a service job. If you look at rents in Roxbury, your $18 an hour doesn't put you in a strong financial position in terms of being able to rent. There are things that people can and are doing to fight against the escalation, but some in the city—and I'm one of those—feel that the main tool to change the financial situation is one that we don't control, and that is a financial recession. Then, the amount of money developers have will level off."

When Dylan transferred from Camden College to the University of California at Berkeley, in the 1980s, he finally started understanding class well enough to see gentrification and also his place in the order of things as a young white kid, spawned from "a monk and a hippie." He was living in Oakland, which was still many years away from its extreme tech employee-driven gentrification in the Bay Area, but Berkeley was also having its own struggles with the university tearing down historic homes to build student apartments. In the 1970s, residents enacted two preservation ordinances and fought for rent control, which helped for a time. But UC-Berkeley is similar to other universities across the country that over time have used their clout and real estate holdings to create "revitalized" urban zones. In 2013, the *Baltimore Sun* published a piece detailing how its city universities are trying different models to encourage local retail growth in a way that they claimed benefitted members of the community and the university.[22] "Eds and meds," or universities and the healthcare industry, as cited by a University of Pennsylvania professor in the article, are seen by city planners as the new anchors of economic development in a city, especially those that lost manufacturing as a base.

Education choices are posited as a series of individual choices. What type of school to send a kid to, how to sustain yourself in grad school, where to go to college? But the extent to which those choices are based in beliefs about race and poverty formed by systemic oppression is something that everyone is forced to reckon with.

In Lexington, the majority of white parents we knew managed to get their children into a magnet public school close to UK. The school districted for our neighborhood, William Wells Brown Elementary School—named after the country's first African-American novelist—had a building less than 10 years old and was made up of almost all low-income black kids and a small number of low-income white kids. Other parents chose private schools; people we knew sent their kids to specialized co-op schools, which require that as a parent you spend time working onsite in the classroom. New, individual Montessori programs and preschools also started sprouting up in the downtown area in the three years that I lived there. There were no high schools downtown when we moved to the neighborhood, though there used to be—Paul Laurence Dunbar High School. There is a peculiar trend in Lexington where the schools named after the most inspirational figures in black history have very few blacks who attend, with the exception of William

Wells Brown. Eventually, the school district and the University of Kentucky partnered to create a STEAM-based (science, technology, engineering, arts, and math) magnet high school and housed it in a school building that used to be the black elementary school back when the district schools were segregated.

I was excited about the possibility of having a high-quality high school nearby that neighborhood kids could also attend, but instead of thinking about infill or preservation projects for the existing building, the school district spent time redistricting and angling for millions of dollars to build brand-new high schools miles away from our neighborhood. The district claimed that the older elementary school could not be repurposed for structural issues and promised to relocate the STEAM school somewhere on the university's campus.

Because of all the local networking I had done up to that point, in 2016, I was asked by a school board representative to serve as a town hall facilitator during the redistricting process. I listened to and had to write (without interjecting) comments from angry white parent after angry white parent making wild claims about kids on free lunch whose parents allegedly drove Mercedes Benzes. The white parents who claimed it wasn't about race said they didn't want their kids forced to leave their neighborhood friends in order to integrate William Wells Brown or the other schools in the district. These parents were not the ones who lived in my neighborhood, but I remember wishing our parents had come to advocate for the kids in *our* neighborhood, the ones whom these parents were desperate to keep their kids shielded from.

A couple of families we knew made an intentional decision to send their kids to the mostly black, magnet middle school across the street and didn't seem regretful. But for the most part, white people found or created alternative schooling options for their kids—anything, it seemed to avoid sending them to WWB. It was complicated from a historical standpoint. After the district desegregated, black families in the East End didn't like having their kids bused across the city to schools where their children were socially isolated. William Wells was a concession to those families, but the presence of so many low-income students clustered in a school meant it was automatically at a financial disadvantage, even if there were sociocultural advantages that the parents had advocated for.

When public schools lose resources, students who have overwhelming social needs are left behind, the schools don't perform well on state tests, and then even more people shun the school, proscribing the remaining teachers and students to an educational Phantom Zone—a metaphor that's even more accurate than it appears on the surface when considering the position of those schools in the school-to-prison pipeline, where poor students learn little more than how to follow rigid rules that don't enhance learning or creativity.

In *The New Jim Crow*, civil rights lawyer Michelle Alexander explores the roots behind the mass incarceration crisis plaguing black and brown communities across the country. The crisis starts in the schools; harsh punishments for minor infractions that are disproportionately meted out to black and brown children starting as early as preschool. The U.S. Department of Education released a study in 2016 revealing that black students are almost four times more likely to be suspended in preschool as white students are.[23] Those rates continue between kindergarten and 12th grade, with black students more at risk of being arrested for an in-school infraction. Truancy and suspensions also place kids at risk for arrest or criminal activity later in life. It's a vicious cycle that connects education in gentrifying neighborhoods directly to law enforcement, notably anti-black policing.

In the book, Mingus follows this path. He ends up attending a failing neighborhood school and from there it's a relatively short path into his criminal behavior. Arthur Lomb, Dylan and Mingus' other white childhood friend, describes their neighborhood high school, Sarah J. Hale, as a prison. Lomb appeared positioned to attend a magnet school like Stuyvesant, studying all the time and worrying about test scores. He didn't get in, and eventually started selling drugs with Mingus. Dylan, on the other hand, was free.

CHAPTER 6

BROKEN WINDOWS

"I thought it was just one bad cop.... But it's bigger than that.... I'm not strong enough for this."
—SUPERMAN, "Action Comics 43"

Judge, Jury... and No Justice!
(DC Comics Presents #14)

Lethem doesn't go in-depth about the role of the police in Dylan's Brooklyn neighborhood, however, it may just be a reflection of the ways Dylan can evade those interactions due to his race.

In *The Fortress of Solitude*, the police are referenced often from Dylan's naive adolescent point of view, however, they seldom appear in the book interacting with other characters. Dylan and his friends spend most of their time trying to bypass the police—not necessarily by avoiding illegal things, like graffiti tagging buildings and shoplifting the markers and paint necessary to do so, or buying drugs before a concert, but they do these things furtively to avoid police attention. During the climatic and devastating end to the first section of the book, Dylan is quickly spirited from the scene of an incident that would have ruined all of his college and life plans had he been caught by the police. The police hover throughout the novel like spectral beings, seldom seen but evoking fear.

Before and after communities gentrify, poor people deal with presumed criminality, not necessarily because everyone in those communities is doing bad things, but because of a mix of racist policing policies and aforementioned issues like jobs or education that affect how people are able to put food on their table. If people are locked out of legal means to make money, some might resort to illegal jobs, like drug dealing, which can bring a heavy police presence. During the 1980s, police officers called in SWAT teams, who used tanks to bulldoze people's homes as a means of arresting drug dealers and serve warrants. In *The New Jim Crow*, Alexander said that Reagan's War on Drugs contributed to the militarization and escalation of law enforcement tactics in black and brown communities, scaring residents about the implications of crack cocaine so much that in some cases they supported the increased police presence and subsequent mass incarceration of their communities. "At the time (Reagan) declared this new war, less than 2 percent of the American public viewed drugs as the most important issue facing the nation. ... By waging a war on drug users and dealers, Reagan made good on his promise to crack down on the racially defined 'others'—the undeserving."

One thing *The Fortress of Solitude* does is subtly chart the evolution of drug use in America as experienced by Dean Street residents, from the recreational marijuana used by Rachel and Abraham's bohemian friends and Barrett Rude Jr., to Dylan dropping acid or doing mushrooms with his friends, to Barrett and Mingus moving from cocaine to smoking crack. While it's unclear as to whether this progression is a commentary on the War on Drugs, Lethem illustrates drugs' journey across the urban landscape. His book stops before the current epidemic of heroin and opiate-based addiction ravaging majority white communities in this country. Under this new circumstance, the war on drugs has stopped, with requests from lawmakers and law enforcement for compassion and treatment.

Our Lexington neighborhood reflected the heroin epidemic when we first moved in. The corner where our apartment stood was a hot spot for people purchasing heroin, sex or both. As excited as I was about the park across the street, teenagers were always hunched over the playground equipment shooting dice or selling drugs and occasionally shooting each other for the money involved in either. My husband's old car still carries a bullet in the passenger seat after a shootout one day when we had gone biking. Neighbors who moved into a duplex next door were using heroin and there were frequent domestic violence incidents in which the police were called. They were white, and the other white neighbors quickly and steadfastly disavowed them. In fact, the majority of the people buying drugs or sex on our block were white.

The drug war fueled a rise in aggressive policing. The "broken windows" theory of policing, which mandated that police departments treat quality of life crimes as seriously as murder, led to "stop and frisk," the practice of targeting people for random stops or illegal searches. This practice, ruled unconstitutional in 2013, was a way of life in black and brown communities in the Bronx, Harlem, Brooklyn, and New Jersey. Police justified the prejudiced policing by saying that they occasionally found weapons or drugs on people of color, so they should *all* be checked. The policy presumed that most or all black men were criminals. Black men and women jailed as a result of these biased interactions were folded into the mass incarceration crisis plaguing black communities today.

Overpolicing was not just used in the cities. People of color have historically been subjected to police surveillance or incarceration while living or merely passing through suburban communities. "Sundown towns," where African Americans were advised to be out of town "by sundown" or to not "let the sun set on their back," were full of people who brought those hostile mindsets well into the 21st century. Trayvon Martin, the black teenager murdered by white Hispanic security officer George Zimmerman, was initially targeted by Zimmerman for simply returning to his suburban neighborhood. The youth had only walked to the store to get snacks and was walking back home in the dark.

After the murder of teenager Michael Brown in the St. Louis suburb of Ferguson, Missouri—an event that began over an accusation that Brown was jaywalking—a Justice Department investigation found that Ferguson had developed the outrageous habit of generating department revenue through fines and violations targeted overwhelmingly at poor or black citizens. This oppressive, anti-black policing has been in place since before the Civil War, when patrollers—whom it can be argued provided the template for the modern-day U.S. law enforcement model—would see an unaccompanied slave and demand that person's identification, pass, or reason for walking around by themselves. Giving a true or satisfactory answer was not a guarantee against violence or death. That hasn't changed over time.

Even Superman experienced police violence. In 2015, writers introduced a storyline for *Action Comics Number 42*, in which Superman, after losing his alien super powers, stands with a group of protesters—putting his white male-presenting body on the line—who are being confronted by heavily militarized police officers while exercising their right to assembly. Media articles about this particular comic noted the similarities in the protests portrayed in the comic to the real-life Black Lives Matter protests taking place that year over the killings of unarmed black men by the police in Missouri, Baltimore, Maryland,[24] Cincinnati, Ohio,[25] or Madison, Wisconsin.[26, 27]

Growing up, my experiences mirrored Dylan's in that I didn't have much face-to-face contact with police. I had sisters, so my parents only gave us a mild version of "the talk" when we started driving. I imagine they thought our gender might put us less at risk during traffic stops.[28] But male friends and boyfriends were far more specific about what needed to be done in the event of a vehicular interaction. In hindsight, I'm sure it's not an accident that my father was one of the best and most careful drivers I've ever known. For more than 30 years, he had never been pulled over by the police. But we never talked about *why*. Before I moved into a gentrifying neighborhood, I assumed that if I kept my head down and didn't do anything criminal, no one could see me. Glasses on, head down, full-on Clark Kent mode. Living in gentrifying neighborhoods, I felt exposed or visible in a different kind of way. Especially as I watched how my white neighbors engaged the police for nuisances like noise, trash, or code violations.

During the time I lived in Chicago, gentrification in the Lakeview/Boystown neighborhood placed a spotlight on racism in the LGBTQ community. In 2007, a new community center was being built by advocacy organization Center on Halsted. The

175,000-square foot community center was part of a major retail development that is currently the largest LGBT center in the Midwest. It was anchored by a Whole Foods and a health clinic that offered rapid HIV testing, and mental health counseling for people who were coming out or coming to terms with their sexuality. The center opened to much fanfare and positive feedback until large numbers of queer black teens began coming from the south side to hang out at the center and stay in the neighborhood after the center closed at 9 p.m. In a city as segregated as Chicago, the teens were extra visible in that north side neighborhood, and white residents began calling the police on the teens, complaining about noise and even prostitution. Considering that they were teenagers, it bothered me why there wasn't a similar target on white people in the neighborhood who were soliciting minors for sex and exploiting individuals who may have been homeless or housing insecure *because of* their sexuality.

There was a bit too much irony in the fact that these residents, some of whom had perhaps been targets of harassment by police years earlier for being sexual minorities, were now calling the police on younger gay, lesbian and trans people of color. The Lakeview residents chose to side with each other as affluent white neighbors and engage the police in a different way. Given that I can't hide behind my race, I have to be far more careful in the ways that I involve police on behalf of my neighbors or myself.

One night in our Lexington apartment, my husband went to ask our upstairs neighbors to keep the noise down. The neighbors, who were white, had come home from the bar and were throwing an after-party on a weeknight. My stepdaughter was there that night and it was going on 3 a.m. The neighbors rudely refused and we ended up calling the police nonemergency number. When we saw the blue lights pull up outside and my husband went to greet them, it was the first time I was really scared about the implications of having made that call. *What if they thought he was the problem tenant? Would they take our white neighbors' word over ours?* The situation ended without resolution; nothing happened to my husband, our neighbors went back to their apartment after the police left and turned their music up even louder. But it was the first I remember being acutely aware of what it meant to live where we lived being in the skin we were in.

The feelings I had during that interaction were bound in my understanding of the context. We were black people, living in a black neighborhood with drug activity, in an area where things were changing. Our apartment at the time was one that had been bought cheaply and renovated by our landlord; we had been told that the house had previously been abandoned or foreclosed on. In any case, the property valuation administrator website shows that our landlord bought the house in 2008 for $84,000. In 2017, the duplex was worth $220,000. Prior to her purchase, the property was valued at only $15,000. That the area had been hit hard by crime was part of the low housing values—a symptom more than the actual disease. At that time, Lexington wasn't known for having lots of murders like larger cities, though drug-related offenses in the neighborhood like prostitution and burglary were common. But the larger force driving the low property values was not an accident.

CHAPTER 7

CONTAINMENT

The Power and the Choice!
(Action Comics #504)

Housing policy is the third Big Bad and perhaps the hardest to face, because the rules are woven so intricately into so many aspects of society. So many people and institutions depend on these policies; to a certain extent, they keep the economy afloat and continue the cycle of gentrification.

Segregated housing policy was codified over time by invested stakeholders. According to Beryl Satter's book *Family Properties: Race, Real Estate, and the Exploitation of Black Urban America*, "in 1924, the National Association of Real Estate Boards adopted the [Chicago Real Estate Board]'s code of refusing to sell to blacks outside of specific areas. Real estate boards across the nation recognized CREB's pioneering work in maintaining all-white communities and looked to CREB for advice as they crafted their own racially restrictive plans." Satter's book revealed that NAREB had assistance with what she calls "black containment" from the Federal Housing Administration, which looked at the maps and neighborhood lines drawn by organizations like NAREB and its local counterparts, and used that information to determine where African Americans would be likely to live, using that information to not just corral black people within those areas but also deny those neighborhoods mortgage insurance, making the barriers to entry extremely high (buying a house in cash) or consigning most of the people to rental agreements. Real estate-adjacent workers like landlords used this information to line their own pockets, knowing that African Americans were restricted to certain areas with a finite amount of housing. This caused much of the overcrowding seen in Northern cities during the Great Migration, as restricted neighborhoods strained to hold not just the black people born there, but the trainloads of black people arriving every day from Mississippi, the Carolinas, Tennessee, Alabama, Georgia, Florida and Texas. The overcrowding and lack of maintenance from landlords created slums, which then intensified poverty and created conditions likely for crime, which then brought more police.

Financial institutions used the redlining data to determine mortgage approvals and interest rates. Black people with good credit were charged excessively high interest rates, or rates consistent with being a high-risk borrower, even if they were not. After the 2008 housing collapse, it was discovered that black people with good credit were more often steered toward risky or "subprime" mortgages that had odd financing structures. Borrowers thought they were getting a good deal, and more often than not, would later be faced with skyrocketing interest rates after a short period of time. Elderly people—those who had managed despite the hurdles erected by NAREB to purchase homes and pay their mortgages in full—were swindled by shady financial companies that took their paid-for homes and put reverse mortgages on them, which gave short-term cash to people on a fixed income but also put their homes at risk of foreclosure.

Segregated housing policies allowed white families to increase their wealth up to 400 times more than black or brown families, because their homes were appraised at higher values for living in non-redlined areas. Other industries took their cues from these biased policies. Neighborhoods with large numbers of black or brown people became known as "food deserts," because they lacked any decent grocery stores for miles; people generally had to leave their neighborhoods and travel far away for food or they overpaid for processed, occasionally spoiled food at corner stores that had more variety of alcohol or cigarettes than fruits or vegetables. Major retailers generally ignored redlined areas. You were unlikely to see retailers like Target or the Old Navy set up locations there. Car insurance, much like the mortgage insurance, is many times higher in these areas because of perceived crime. When I moved to Old Town in Chicago, I gave up my car after a couple of months, but not before noticing that my insurance rates had decreased significantly upon moving to the majority white Near North Side.

In the 21st century, redlining even has a digital component. In March 2017, a report by the National Digital Inclusion Alliance showed that AT&T had been engaging in "digital discrimination"; the telecommunications company had intentionally declined to update broadband infrastructure in low-income Cleveland neighborhoods.[29] When overlaying those areas with maps showing redlining, those neighborhoods lacking broadband also happened to be largely African American. Internet speeds and phone reception were worse there than in more affluent, whiter West Side neighborhoods or inner-ring suburbs.

Much of American wealth-building is still tied to real estate—even after the housing meltdown. Neighborhoods that had previously been redlined and appraised as being lower in value are, in some areas, now worth 10 times their 20th century values, and whiteness plays a large role in making that possible.

Whiteness by itself isn't enough. Dylan waited for the Solver girls to return to Dean Street and they never did, and Dean Street remained static throughout most of his childhood. But whiteness plus the generational or professional wealth that allows white people to purchase a lot of property and renovate it, helped along by businesses and individuals who cater to that presence, pushes the bar toward gentrification. Whiteness plus the ability to navigate educational systems or create exclusive ones pushes the bar further. Whiteness with both of those things multiplied by the ever-present discomfort around or fear of black and brown people that spurs engagement with police to monitor or contain them can lurch forward a process that there is no turning back from. As a college-educated black woman, I shift in and out of these categories easily (or uneasily) depending on the situation, understanding the things that mark me as privileged, but also painfully aware of what does and doesn't matter to anyone who sees me sitting on my front porch.

Being a homeowner appears on the outside to be the sum of a million individual choices, but those choices are all formed by larger systemic forces. The choices are informed by The Lie and affect the ways that Dylan or I attempt to build a home or find a community. Re-reading over *The Fortress of Solitude*, I think it's one of the many reasons Dylan ran away; he knew that everything churning below the surface on Dean Street was bigger than his will to challenge it. The challenges are why I stay in the city and make my home there.

CHAPTER 8

GOTTA HAVE IT

Creative Differences
(Superman: The Man of Steel #85)

The *Fortress of Solitude* was the first art I experienced as an adult that referenced gentrification explicitly. In the aughts, as the phenomenon grew more widespread in tandem with rising income inequality, there were straightforward, earnest depictions of white people trying to make it in cities and neighborhoods where the people of color are relegated to the background or erased, like the much-discussed HBO comedy *Girls*, which situated a quartet of exceptionally privileged young white women living in the majority-black Bedford-Stuyvesant neighborhood of Brooklyn.

An early episode centered around the girls going to a party in Bushwick and one accidentally smokes crack, playing up for laughs the idea that the characters are having an adventure in this "rough" (read: black) neighborhood that hasn't gentrified yet. Or there are satires such as *Portlandia* that make fun of certain aspects of gentrification or stereotypes of urban residents—again, revolving around white people—like long brunch lines, overly aggressive, bodily modified bike deliverymen, or tech culture workplaces where people play competitive hide-and-go seek.

The 2016 HBO series *Insecure*, which was set in Los Angeles and created by Senegalese-American writer Issa Rae, did subtly reference the occurrence of upwardly mobile black people living in close proximity to lower-income ones. College-educated characters Issa and her live-in boyfriend Lawrence, the latter an aspiring app developer, live in an apartment complex next to a member of the Bloods gang who hates the rival Crips so much he refuses to allow anyone to say any words with the letter C in them when he's around. The show's second season more directly addressed gentrification, beginning with the main character learning that a new developer had taken over her apartment complex, and ending the season with her being forced to move, and walking through her changing neighborhood full of buildings for lease and jogging white people.

The Public Broadcasting Service's long-running, critically acclaimed show *Sesame Street* inadvertently touched on the impact of gentrification when in 2015, after 45 years on the air, it declared that the premium cable network HBO would be distributing the show and airing new episodes behind its paywall. The format and production had changed a year prior: it was cut down from an hour to 30 minutes; focused more on the puppets and animated characters instead of inter-actions between the other human characters; and also changed the set. The original 1969 set mirrored urban neighborhoods in New York City, with trash cans on the street, laundry hanging on lines between buildings and kids on the stoop. The new set looks as gentri-fied as any corner in Boerum Hill, with a community garden and Oscar the Grouch popping up next to recycling bins.

In 2016, one of the show's original cast members, Bob McGrath, who plays Bob, announced that he, Roscoe Orman (who plays Gordon) and Emilio Delgado (who plays Luis) had all been let go. The irony was extreme considering that elderly people of color are some of the most vulnerable populations in gentrifying neighborhoods, as they tend to live on fixed incomes and can't readily absorb sharp increases in property taxes, major house repairs needed to keep buildings up to code, or expensive retail shops that spring up to serve newer affluent residents.[30] In an update, Sesame Workshop CEO Jeffrey Dunn said in August 2016 there was a misunderstanding and that cast members would just be in reduced roles, not fired.

According to Ana Petrovic in the *Elder Law Journal*, elderly residents in gentrifying neighborhoods lose access to younger neighbors in their social networks whom they depend on for help with living conditions, medical care and groceries.[31] Elderly residents are also at risk for scams involving their mortgages, as they look for means to supplement their incomes. A con artist in Chicago was convicted in 2016 for tricking elderly homeowners into signing reverse mortgages that totaled $10 million in equity.[32]

I took the *Sesame Street* news personally, as Delano and I had our first child together at that point, and in the mornings I would play for him YouTube videos of *Sesame Street* episodes from the 1970s and 1980s.[33] For my child to see Bob, Linda, Maria, Luis, Gordon, Susan and Olivia *was* the point. What could I tell my kids about their future in a world that would remove its elders without warning or explanation? And what an opportunity the show missed to teach a generation of children to value their elderly neighbors as community assets instead of afterthoughts. It was heartening to read in *The Fortress of Solitude* that Abraham was taking care of Barrett in later years, bringing him food and medicine and keeping him company. In the end, without family around, Barrett had to depend on his neighbors, the ones he barely talked to back in the day.

A couple of television series tackled gentrification in a way that Dylan and Mingus would have appreciated. Streaming service Netflix released two series as part of the Marvel Cinematic Universe where gentrification was a major part of the plot: *Daredevil* (2015) and *Luke Cage* (2016). The shows were set in the Manhattan neighborhoods of Hell's Kitchen and Harlem, respectively, but the underlying themes were the same. Daredevil fought Kingpin, who was buying up property and harassing business owners toward his goal of being, well, a kingpin, but the latter also wanted to forcefully create the type of neighborhood he always wanted to live in and erase the Kitchen's gritty past. Luke Cage fought Black Mariah and Cottonmouth, or *Cornell*, as he would prefer to be known, as the latter two launder drug money and pay off corrupt cops and councilmen—not necessarily to halt gentrification, but to keep white people from being the primary beneficiaries of it. Mariah publicly espouses the cultural history of Harlem as one of black businesses and upward mobility, and she's not above resorting to murder or campaign finance fraud to keep it that way. "For black lives to matter," she said in Episode 1, "black history has to matter as well."

Luke Cage first appeared in 1972, in Marvel Comics' *Hero for Hire* #1. His plot lines were drawn from the era, focusing on gang wars and drugs, but Cage was also a product of the blaxploitation era and that of the Black Panthers. The cynicism of the post-Civil Rights Era had set in, riots leveled whole neighborhoods from Los Angeles to the Bronx, and black people were disproportionately suffering from economic crises and unemployment that unraveled gains they thought they had made. The Panthers and blaxploitation flicks provided alternative narratives in which black people had self-determination and the ability to fight the societal issues plaguing their communities, in addition to fighting other black people who were tearing down the black community, like drug dealers, pimps, and people who were selling out for The Man.

By bringing gentrification into the discussion—and anti-black violence with Cage wearing a hoodie in homage to Trayvon Martin—Black Mariah and Cottonmouth become slightly more nuanced. They're criminals but focused on property ownership and economic uplift in a historically black neighborhood. In a comic-tragic scene, during Season 1, episode 5 ("Just to Get a Rep"), one of Cottonmouth's flunkies says he's been reading up on the politics and the conditions that led to the rise of hip hop. He references the Dodgers leaving Brooklyn, Bob Moses' freeway plans and harmful urban development, white flight and the infamous Daniel Moynihan report, where the sociologist suggested a "benign neglect" of the public reckoning with race.[34] Cottonmouth angrily shoots his employee in the head for a similar suggestion of benign neglect toward Luke Cage, but the scene deftly ties together these interrelated events, situating the show and its plot in important historical context.

Cage, as portrayed by Mike Colter, is also shown as being a lover of literature, reading books such as *Fist Stick Knife Gun* by Geoffrey Canada, the founder of the Harlem Children's Zone, who Cottonmouth references as a model for Mariah because of the former's role in gentrifying certain areas of Harlem; *Playing the Numbers: Gambling in Harlem Between the Wars* by Shane White; Ralph Ellison's *Invisible Man*, where Harlem features prominently; and *Can't Stop, Won't Stop* by Jeff Chang, the book that Cottonmouth's associate was reading.

In 2017, Brooklyn-born director Spike Lee focused his nostalgia for a pre-gentrification Fort Greene on a Netflix show based on his 1986 first full-length film "She's Gotta Have It," with the same title. The new Nola Darling managed to reference gentrification and rent prices every episode. Episode 9 was actually titled "Gentrification." While the show received mixed reviews, the most poignant part of the production was the opening credits with photo stills of 1970s Fort Greene—when it was mostly black and Latinx—juxtaposed with the gleaming, chrome contemporary Fort Greene, with white yuppies and their strollers featured prominently throughout the show.

Superman's Justice League associate Batman/Bruce Wayne had a case in which he reflected on the role that housing policy, policing and segregation have on a murder case he is following up on in "A Simple Case" (#44). It is worth noting that when he explores this, Batman, much like Superman in *Action Comics 42*, is able to come to a higher point of understanding about these complex social issues when he is stripped of his superhero powers and standing. Taking off the mask and having their privileges taken away allows them to empathize with people in the community in a different way. It opens a door to multiple truths.

The issue's storyline follows a flashback device on the killing of a young boy; the cartoonists rendered certain panels in shades of gray to underpin the moral ambiguity of all of the involved parties. Snippets of fictional news reports are interspersed in the background of the panels—they are from Bruce Wayne's recollection but they also serve as Gotham City's institutional memory. The issue takes on Gotham's segregated housing, fortified by racial covenants, slum neighborhoods, anti-black policing in those same neighborhoods, and the new Wayne Apartments eventually going up in the area that drove out longtime residents, including the one whose murder he was trying to solve. The latter implicates himself in the neighborhood's gentrification and possibly the boy's murder.

That detail that resonated with me: that we are all implicated in the cycle of gentrification to some extent. When we try to search for a home or a community, the decisions we make, or that we think we make, so many of them have already been made for us. By the time we "choose" a neighborhood or a school, or whether to call the police versus the city's non-emergency number or walk into the fancy hipster restaurant selling "fusion" dim sum over the mom-and-pop Chinese restaurant up the street, we're reacting to a script that's already been written. It's only through social mobility—that ability to slip through worlds, like Dylan as an adult, or Superman, or me and my family—that those options broaden. But some factors never change; the level of visibility in a given community is always ambiguous, especially as a black gentrifier.

PART III
GOING TO WAR

——————

Pissed

One night, during a block club meeting down at the community development organization office on the west side of Cleveland, a white man with an angry face pushed a grainy, blown-up photograph around the table. It was a photo of a dark-skinned man, standing in an alley with his back turned to the camera. "See, this is what I was talking about, stuff like this and I'm fed up with it," he said. I waited for the man to elaborate, but he did not. I looked at the photocopy. The archivist in me went straight to a technical description: *A man with his back turned. The man appears to have dark skin. He is standing in a driveway. There is a small garage to his left and a car to his right.* The other attendees of the block club meeting—all white except for me in a neighborhood that, according to the 2010 Census is at least 36 percent black and 13 percent Hispanic—looked down too. I held the photo up to my face. What did they see? What was I missing? The block club president spoke up. "I'm sorry," he said, sounding a bit exasperated, "What are we looking at?"

"He's urinating in the driveway," the angry man answered, practically apoplectic in his response.

This was not the first time I'd heard this type of complaint at this type of meeting. This seemed like a relatively minor thing to be worked up about, not to mention the fact that Angry Man had taken a photo of a private citizen minding his business and implied his criminality. Even as a homeowner, I couldn't summon the amount of rage this man was expressing over a little bit of urine. In the city, urine happens sometimes. For me, public urination ranks lower than the pigeons painting our driveway with bird shit thick as oil paint. But he went on and on in a way that was familiar to me from living in other gentrified neighborhoods. He was already conducting routine, unauthorized surveillance. There was another man at the meeting who I recognized from his Nextdoor post as saying he'd followed some black teens down the street whom he suspected to be burglars.

The big topic of discussion that night was a corner store at the end of our block, where Angry Man alleged that an excessive amount of crime was taking place: drug deals, overdoses, prostitution, even burglaries that he wanted to pin on the corner store's clientele, which he couldn't prove. "I mean, have you seen those people," he asked rhetorically, "They're really undesirable."

The block club president, a friendly, white gay man who worked for the community development organization, frowned at that statement. "I don't know if I get what you're saying, but I'm concerned that you're talking about people who live in our neighborhood who use this store regularly," he told Angry Man.

And of course, this was *exactly* the issue. But no one else from the neighborhood who uses the store was at the meeting.

I tried to imagine what it would have been like if any of *The Fortress of Solitude* characters had shown up to the meeting. Barrett would probably not have come, before or after his addiction, but mostly because he was a celebrity and had little interest in anyone else lacking that designation. Abraham would have passed, probably with excuses about finishing his film. I'd like to think an adult Henry would have shown up. Real estate owner Arthur Lomb would have likely have been a topic of discussion, even in his absence, as he took up Isabel Vendle's machine/mantle. What would the adult Dylan would have done? Would he have been as uncomfortable or upset as I was about the implication that a random black man was singled out as an alleged criminal? Would he have said something? Or would he have stayed silent, complicit? Would he have piped up with suggestions about closed circuit cameras or feel-good motions about directing people to call the city's non-emergency police number for any complaints? Would he have condescendingly referred to himself as a "pioneer" in the neighborhood? Rachel Ebdus probably would've pounded the table and called Angry Man what he was: racist.

Neighborhood associations or block clubs play a critical role in gentrification and as an expression of class privilege. As a young girl, I knew of them during visits to Chicago to my grandmother's South Side Chatham neighborhood. Chatham was a solidly black middle-class neighborhood; gospel singer Mahalia Jackson lived three blocks from my grandmother's house, as did various black doctors, lawyers and entrepreneurs. But this wasn't an accident; in a city as segregated as Chicago, middle-class black neighborhoods had ways of replicating the same exclusionary tactics that existed in white neighborhoods. In Chatham, South Shore, Auburn-Gresham and Pill Hill, hand-painted signs appeared on block after block with a list of rules. "*No car washing in the street, no loud music/radios, no loitering, no speeding, no littering/trash, no horn blowing.*" etc. No one had signs like this where I lived in Milwaukee. As a kid, I always wondered if it meant you'd be taken to jail if you broke the rules.

In *The New Urban Renewal: The Economic Transformation of Harlem and Bronzeville*, sociologist Derek Hyra said "Intra-racial class conflict arises when competing factions, such as homeowners and renters, debate the path of neighborhood development." In the Bronzeville neighborhood of Chicago, where my father grew up, for instance, ongoing gentrification led by homeowner-dominated block clubs are pushing for higher property values that would explicitly exclude low-income black people. By this logic, if my father had not managed to move upward from the class status he grew up in, he wouldn't have been welcome in his own birthplace 50 years later.

A 1957 scholarly article by former Chicago Urban League Community Organization Director Alva B. Maxey in *The Block Club Movement in Chicago* said that, "block clubs are attempting to teach people to (1) develop and maintain cleanliness, (2) subdue, restrain and sublimate their hostilities (3) assume their proportionate share of civic responsibility, (4) be thrifty and dependable, (5) develop aesthetic tastes with regard to their surroundings, (6) adopt and extend good manners, (7) strive for upward mobility by conforming to prevailing norms of behavior, and (8) learn the ways to become acceptable to a diverse urban population. Thus these organizations are striving to educate their members and neighbors in the direction of middle class ideals."

Maxey experienced gentrification firsthand; she and her husband waged a very public fight to save their Bronzeville home from demolition as part of a public housing expansion.[35] However, her view on block clubs was steeped in respectability politics and the Talented Tenth ideals of the era. If we are nice enough, if we display good manners, if we perform the right white upper middle class cues, then we'll eventually be accepted as equals. I don't know that Isabel Vendle as characterized would have ever found any "acceptable" people of color. She strikes me as having been unapologetically interested in white families only, and her thoughts about Dylan attending public school, or her comments about the other neighbors seem to underscore this.

As an adult, block clubs came to signify something entirely different to me. Because I wanted to be proactive and involved in my neighborhood, I joined the neighborhood association when I lived in Lexington. Many of the people on the board, including me, lived on Johnson Avenue. Again, in a neighborhood that was more than 50 percent African American, the board consisted of people who did not grow up in the neighborhood, including myself, and except for myself were all white. Whenever we held our meetings, I noticed that attendance was always higher if we had the police liaison on the agenda or were doing updates on "safety," and the attendees, outside of board members, were generally white people who were new to the neighborhood.

In Lexington, I felt like my neighbors, especially the ones on Johnson Avenue meant well. We had made friends with many of the people on our block, visited each other's homes, watched each other's children, fed each other, talked with each other. It was truly a village where I felt as though I could get some of those opposing viewpoints across and where, as time went on, white neighbors actively stood in solidarity to proclaim that black lives matter. I could say "*Hey, can we pull together a coat drive for neighborhood kids since winters here are getting colder, instead of focusing on a food truck event this month*" without worrying that anyone would find fault in the logic or get defensive. In Cleveland, the neighborhood block club actually has the word "Brigade" in its title, which means "*a large body of military troops in tactical formation*," and that feels like a depressingly apt summation of how gentrification plays out in bigger cities.

Gentrification is so often about going to war against poor people, old people, black or brown people, or immigrants. And frequently, actual military tools are used in this fight. Excessive and aggressive anti-black policing for minor quality-of-life infractions. Law enforcement-type surveillance, from closed circuit cameras on people's front porches to people like Angry Man who were actively spying on neighbors and photographing them in and outside of their homes. Angry Man took "brigade" to heart.

The tools reflect the world we live in, so there are digital apps employed in this race and class-tinged theater. The Nextdoor social media app started in 2011 as a way of bringing new urban neighbors together. A user could send invites to everyone on their block and then share messages with each other about yard sales, local events, or crime. Mostly it was crime, or the people who were perceived as criminals. Users and nonusers began complaining that Nextdoor was being used to engage in racial profiling. Users would share messages about people of color walking down the street who were presumed to be casing houses for robbery, but they either lived in the neighborhood or were going to visit friends. Nextdoor's developers adjusted the front-end design to try and mitigate racial profiling. Users who wanted to describe a crime or people thought to be criminals would be asked very detailed questions before being allowed to identify people by race, and without this series of identifications the user's post would not be published. Users quickly circumvented this by simply shortening "black" or "African American" to "AA" in their postings, so that the algorithms wouldn't pick it up. I know because those are the same messages I see in my neighborhood's Nextdoor comments.

Other tools include the weight of law or policy. Eminent domain takes land or real estate away from private individuals for development. Code enforcement on cosmetic external property issues drives up punitive fines that could force eviction or short sale from someone on a fixed income. It's war, pure and simple.

Being a black woman in a gentrified neighborhood often feels like I'm fighting behind enemy lines, in which case, my home becomes my fortress of solitude, the place I use to hide or recharge from always having the legitimacy of my personhood questioned. I'm not interested in Angry Man or his threats to start a petition to get all the bodegas in the district to stop selling alcohol. I'm there for the man photographed in the alley, whose face doesn't get to be seen, who wasn't given a voice in this forum. He's invisible because people only see what they want to see.

CHAPTER 9

VISIBILITY

With This Ring…
(Superman Vol. 2 #168)

Harlem Renaissance author Ralph Ellison's seminal work *Invisible Man* describes a nameless protagonist who is never truly seen as a human being, only as a template for other people to paint their stereotypes and misconceptions. He is a respectability politics-playing college kid. He's a union scab. He's a country boy in the big city. He's a militant. He's a sellout. He's an exotic black lover. He's a ghost. He moves through his Harlem neighborhood, haunting its corners until, weary of it all, he moves underground and lives beneath the throb and thrum of the city, stealing electricity and listening to jazz, living an improvisational life.

Despite critics' assertions that the ring/Aeroman plot in the book was a distraction—magical realism shoehorned into a text that is otherwise extraordinarily down-to-earth—I like the ways that *The Fortress of Solitude*'s characters use Aaron X. Doily's ring to play with invisibility. For Dylan, the ring's power of invisibility is about being seen differently. It's about power given, as opposed to the power denied for Ellison's protagonist. Dylan's use of the ring mirrors Superman's use of his Clark Kent persona. Clark is Superman's exact opposite: someone weak, wimpy and awkward, and based in an understanding of what Earthlings—or more concretely, Americans—view as strength. The Kent camouflage lets him play with ideas or presentations of power and belonging. He can fit into American society only by adopting a persona of weakness or incompetence.

Dylan played with power as Aeroman time and again. Using the ring to become Aeroman, he could transcend what he felt were the limitations of race within his neighborhood. He could escape his *whiteboy* identity through flight and become untouchable. His is an inversion of an actual superhero's mantra, which is to run toward danger. Again and again, Dylan runs away, from his neighborhood and himself.

Dylan leaves Aeroman behind in college, as whiteness becomes the default of his social life. He chose a minstrel approximation of Mingus as a different type of costume, one that ironically contrasted him further among the whiteness of his peers. In college, pretending to be tough, he was perceived by his classmates to be truly authentic by being his most fake. Dylan's classmates were marginally in on this deception, feeling like proximity to him was potentially as close to someone "street" (read: black) as they were going to get, and also using him to assuage their class guilt.

When Dylan returns to the ring, there's no cape or mask involved, but it does allow him invisibility, perhaps as a commentary white privilege. That Dylan could walk into a prison as a white man and be granted access without being seen works as a statement on the default safety granted to the identity or presentation of whiteness, to the point where the many systems of oppression that hold white supremacy in place become invisible. It's a compelling inversion of Ellison's assertion, that racial identity makes us invisible in different ways.

In gentrified landscapes I'm often an abstraction, where people who look like Dylan become the default—the rule and not the exception. When we first moved to Cleveland, for instance, I was a stay-at-home mom for eight months. But black women, often denigrated as bad or dysfunctional mothers, are never seen as stay-at-home moms. That's a title with connotations for more affluent (white) women. At grocery stores or other retail locations, customer or public service workers—including the librarians with whom I share professional affiliation—spoke to me in such a way that assumed that I was poor, revealing how they feel poor people should be treated in public spaces. It was as though I had failed a test I didn't know I was taking. If I signed my son up for a class at the art museum, the other moms always looked at me skeptically, as though I had come in off the street and snuck into the class. People assumed I was unmarried even though I wear a ring. I'd get questions about "my baby's father" instead of "my husband," as though everyone was walking around with a copy of the Moynihan Report in their back pocket. If I went to a neighborhood meeting, white people would look at me suspiciously until I started talking. There's always a pause—a dip in the conversation or a chill in the social atmosphere—where I can tell people are surprised. *"Oh, she's articulate."* When people would find out where we live, I can see them doing the math in their head, and see the slow, up and down appraisal: *"What do you do that you could buy that house?"* Which is usually followed by a very direct: *"Where do you work,"* or *"What do you do?"* How I'm physically seen varies in different situations.

When I was living in Boston and walking around at night by myself in gentrifying neighborhoods, I would usually try and follow (not too closely behind) another person on the street for my own safety. I startled more than one white male this way, even if I was a block behind them, but I don't know that it ever occurred to them that I was a young woman just trying to be safe and visible against whatever might go bump in the night.

One evening a white neighbor in Lexington looked right through me, and then once he acknowledged my physical body, he moved nervously to the corner of the sidewalk. This was only two days after we had attended the neighborhood association meeting and talked about attending the same Big 10 university for undergrad. But in this instance, he literally didn't see *me*.

A recurring insult that enraged my husband was when he'd take our kids out for breakfast at a local diner in Lexington (the staff were always super sweet and welcoming), and white patrons would accuse him of stealing our son's stroller when it was time to leave, or insist that he must have been grabbing someone else's stroller by accident. Taken individually, it's easy to wonder if you imagined the moment or read a person's response incorrectly. But the separate incidents pancake atop one another, a sticky mess that stays with you long after you've tried to digest it.

Poet Claudia Rankine described similar microaggressions in *Citizen: An American Lyric*. "Each moment is like this—before it can be known, categorized as similar to another thing and dismissed, it has to be experienced, it has to be seen. What did he just say? Did she really just say that? Did I hear what I think I heard? Did that just come out of my mouth, his mouth, your mouth? The moment stinks." It always felt like the assumption was that as black people we weren't supposed to be in a gentrifying neighborhood; that people who looked like us were on the way out, not settling in and planting roots.

To white people in the neighborhood who didn't know me, I was as invisible and malleable as Ellison's protagonist. I'm a ghost, haunting the block until someone more desirable can buy me out. I'm a data point to prove that the neighborhood is "authentic" or "diverse." To black people still in the neighborhood,

I'm highly visible, the same way that Dylan's family was originally visible to Isabel Vendle. And to be honest, I craved the acknowledgement.

As a Midwest-raised girl, I was always taught to speak to any black people I saw out in the community or on the job, the general idea being that in certain places we were so rare we should always acknowledge each other. Living in black and brown communities I had visibility among people who looked like me, even if it was clear that I wasn't from that specific city. If our eyes meet at work or on the street, I'm speaking or nodding or smiling at you.

One thing I observed with was that in certain settings, that level of visibility was applied differently. Gentrification of our Lexington neighborhood begat patios for outdoor dining. As the numbers of white people in the neighborhood increased, I started seeing more panhandlers out and about—white and black—hitting up brunchers or drinkers in the neighborhood. Sometimes it was the young kids selling candy bars for unspecified sports fundraisers. Sometimes it was older individuals asking for any spare bills or food. If they were black, they'd catch my eye but not ask me for anything. Sometimes if I was by myself, someone black might ask me for something. If I had it, I gave it. If I didn't have it, I'd simply apologize and keep it moving without any harassment. My social mobility had more elasticity in this situation than Dylan, who came to feel like the panhandling requests were a trap, an unwinnable game. If a kid from around the way asked if Dylan had any money on him and Dylan gave it up, he was weak, an easy mark. If Dylan says no, he's implicitly racist because the person doing the asking was black. His frustration about being yoked seemed to be not just a surface concern of bullying, but that in his neighborhood, it always came with this underlying racial tension. And to a certain extent, it involves black people picking up on and playing with white people's fear, turning white people's fear into an expression of situational power for black people. That power is fleeting when considering that white people's fear could lead to a 911 call that ends in a black person's death.[36]

For Dylan, finding the ring was about power through flight or invisibility. Matters of choice. But as a black woman, I know that true power is in visibility. In being seen as my authentic self.

CHAPTER 10

INVISIBILITY

A Place Between
(*Superman Unchained #5*)

For the millions of people who have no home, gentrification is directly responsible for their (in)visibility. The character of Aaron X. Doily—a homeless man in *The Fortress of Solitude*—is a statement about the ways in which gentrification asks us to become blind to others' humanity.

Doily is introduced as a remarkable man, someone who Dylan glimpses as *flying*, not falling, off a building. By page 134, Doily is "fouled in himself, baked in vomit and urine and sweat, his pants black with it," sleeping in the street, with a makeshift cape under his chin. This is also during the time period in which New York's homeless population exploded as the result of several colliding factors: the city nearly had to file for bankruptcy in the 1970s, there was a national recession, and the city was suffering from the municipal de-investment of benign neglect. There was no money to pay the basic bills, let alone money for programs that would have addressed homelessness or its root causes of unemployment: lack of affordable housing, mental health care services, or addiction counseling. Doily is a shorthand, a snapshot of the era.

Lethem addresses the gentrification of Gowanus directly, juxtaposing the new development with the image of Doily as an "alcoholic coma victim" on the street in plain sight. The neighborhood is on the way up; who is letting this man stay in the streets like this? "Is it because he's black," the third-person narrator wondered.

Not quite, I would answer.

One of the things about gentrification I witnessed over and over again is how it attempts to remove poor or vulnerable people from public view. Police calls about panhandling or public intoxication serve to remove those groups off of the street and out of physical sight. News media have documented exclusionary or "defensive" architecture such as spikes in corners of buildings or benches with rolled edges and armrests to prevent homeless people from sleeping on them. *LAist* ran a piece in 2016 about "gentrification fences," a mid-modern-derived wooden slat fence that stops people from looking in, but also closes off a view of anything happening outside of your house or backyard, giving newcomers an intentional bubble to wrap themselves in.[37]

A 2015 piece by Alex Andreao in *The Guardian* about defensive architecture said "City planners work very hard to keep [poverty] outside our field of vision. It is too miserable, too dispiriting, too painful to look at someone defecating in a park or sleeping in a doorway and think of him as 'someone's son.' It is easier to see him and ask only the unfathomably self-centered question: 'How does his homelessness affect me?' So we cooperate with urban design and work very hard at not seeing, because we do not want to see."[38]

In every city I ever lived in, if I were approached for money and I didn't have it, I'd say so, but honestly and with respect enough to look that person in the eye. That behavior isn't worthy of a gold star. But invisibility means that so many people don't get even that base level of acknowledgment. Respect costs nothing. When I lived in Chicago, there were homeless people I regularly gave money, food or spare CTA cards to when I had them, mostly because we would see and talk to each other every day. We were a part of each other's landscape.

But poverty makes people uncomfortable. Stark reminders about the gaps between the rich and poor are jarring, mostly, because they force people to acknowledge how fucked up everything is. People have to acknowledge the lies we've told ourselves about American exceptionalism. I've heard parents admonish their children to look away from an unkempt person holding a cup, seen people look straight ahead through their car windshield, past or away from the person walking by through the street, asking for spare change.

I don't know if the answer about Aaron X. Doily being ignored in the street is because he was black. In Lexington, almost every panhandler or person sifting through the trash I saw was white and public policy seemed to want them to disappear too. Shortly after I left Lexington, controversy erupted over a panhandling measure; the city had banned the act in 2007 and the state supreme court overturned it in 2016. While living there, I remember people complaining in letters to the editor at the *Lexington Herald-Leader* about the line of homeless men and women snaking around the block for the free meal program that would set up in front of the public library on weekends. When I worked at the public library's downtown branch, I met quite a few patrons whose only identification was a day pass from a local homeless shelter. But Lexington is also small enough that I also ran into those same patrons while they were working at their jobs. Some of them worked multiple jobs but couldn't afford a place to live in the city. Those are the truly invisible homeless—people who are priced out of homes or can't find affordable or low-income housing, a situation that gentrification is directly responsible for and exacerbates.

Few people want to acknowledge that aspect of homelessness—that it's not due to a personal or moral failing. There are people who work who can't afford a place to live because wages are too low and the cost of a personal fortress of solitude is prohibitively high. Sociologist Matthew Desmond's 2016 book *Evicted* was a searing indictment on the rental housing industry in America—using my hometown of Milwaukee as a case study—and the ways it impacts poor people. There are children who don't have a secure place to live, but they might not be in a shelter. They're sleeping on a friend's couch or squatting in a building with no windows or heat. Gentrification encourages turning a blind eye to the issue, to refuse to see people and deny them that little bit of humanity.

Maybe Doily eventually had trouble flying with the ring because he was black. Systemic oppression has always made it harder for us to take flight from our circumstances, to leave by choice. "Cain't fight the *air waves*," he whispered when he told Dylan to take the ring. Maybe for Doily, the ring was always about invisibility, which was why he laid in the street for so long before anyone came to his aid.

As I thumbed through my dog-eared copy of *Invisible Man* while thinking about it in relation to *The Fortress of Solitude*, I kept coming back to this quote in the introduction: "There is still available that fictional *vision* of an ideal democracy in which the actual combines with the ideal and gives us representations of a state of things in which the highly placed and the lowly, the black and the white, the northerner and the southerner, the native-born and the immigrant are combined to tell us of transcendent truths and possibilities," Ellison said in an introduction to *Invisible Man*.

Maybe a good book can show us the way.

PART IV
ALIEN

———

Welcome to the City of Tomorrow

(Superman: Metropolis #1)

In 1933, two young Jewish men living in a large immigrant community on Cleveland's east side decided to create a comic book hero who reflected their outsider status.[39] Their superhero was also an immigrant—a refugee to be more specific—from a destroyed planet. He had bulletproof skin and was "more powerful than a locomotive." Wearing the disguise of a "mild-mannered reporter," the alien went by the name Clark Kent. Jerry Siegel and Joe Shuster named their creation Superman and sold him to DC Comics in 1938.[40]

Georgia Tech professor Todd Michney uncovered a bit of history that was news to me while researching the history of Cleveland, and I was fortunate enough to hear him expound on it at a local reading for his book *Surrogate Suburbs: Black Upward Mobility and Neighborhood Change in Cleveland, 1900-1980*. The

Glenville neighborhood that was home to Siegel and Shuster was one of a small number of majority Jewish east side neighborhoods with progressive home owners and activists who would sell homes to African Americans throughout the early 20th century. Jewish families, who in some areas had been subjected to similarly restrictive housing covenants, purchased homes in Glenville before deed restrictions could be put in place. This opened the door for black home-owners, leading to pockets of black upward mobility in Cleveland.

Almost 70 years later, a young black man from an all-white suburb in Northeast Ohio, who was in his senior year of college at the University of Akron, pledged the oldest black fraternity in the country, Alpha Phi Alpha, an organization started in 1906 as a brotherhood of service and safety for other black men at an all-white university. As was customary, everyone on the line received a nickname. This young man, whose major was journalism and was the editor-in-chief of the campus newspaper *The Buchtelite*, was given the name Clark Kent. He even had the glasses. But he was no weakling.

The first time I talked to that man was during a conference in 2011 at a hotel bar in Philadelphia. I thought he was pretty super. A few weeks after we met, I sent him a couple of panels from Superman #268.[41] Luckily, we hit it off better than Clark and Barbara Gordon did.

By 2016, we had been living together as a blended family in Lexington for nearly four years. Our second baby was coming and we had run out of room in our home, had flat salaries and no money to finish renovations on the second floor of the house. My husband started looking for other jobs and was offered a job at a television station in Cleveland. Ohio-born sports superhero LeBron James had returned to play for the Cleveland Cavaliers and my husband was starting his job just in time to cover the NBA finals. We spent Mother's Day weekend looking at houses in the Cleveland area. Our initial searches took us into the inner-ring suburb of Cleveland Heights, where we saw homes and lots twice as big as anything we could afford in Lexington. We didn't find anything that weekend, or the weekend after that.

We continued to search, but most of the houses needed major projects done. After our work on the Lexington house, we just wanted to be able to move into something and not worry about it, especially knowing that when we did, there would be a three-week-old baby with us. I didn't want to worry about contractors or paint swatches with a newborn. I saw online a couple of houses in the city of Cleveland that were turnkey properties. But almost everyone we talked to, black and white and our real estate agent, tried to warn us off of living in the city because of the schools.

We put our own house in Lexington up for sale in the meantime. The pervasive effects of discriminatory housing policies and practice meant that in order to prep our home for sale we had to scrub it of any signs of our identity. Away went my collector's copies of *Trace* magazine, the *Vogue* with Michelle Obama on the cover and the Italian *Vogue* issue with all-black models. Down went the Romare Bearden print; our family portraits and my stepdaughter's black dolls went into a plastic bin in the shed. When she asked why, we were blunt. "We have to hide the fact that we're black in order to have a fair chance at selling our home." We talked to her about the Fair Housing Act of 1968, and what it meant in a city like Lexington. We noticed when our realtor took us to view homes in Cleveland Heights or Shaker Heights; white people had their family portraits and hobbies prominently displayed. How must it feel to always be able to yourself, to be the default, the standard, in and out of your fortress?

In the end, gentrification had so changed our neighborhood, with Johnson Avenue as a highly desirable focal point, that the house sold five days after the listing went up.

In June, Hannah-Jones' *Times* magazine piece came out and we asked our realtor to show us one of the Cleveland homes that had come up earlier in our search. One was in an area called the Detroit-Shoreway neighborhood. It is a west side, "changing," historical area. It was near several local theaters (film and stage), coffee shops, restaurants, 100-year-old Catholic churches, and the West Side Market, an indoor public market with stalls of every imaginable food from Ohio vendors. The neighborhood had mostly Italian and Puerto Rican residents, though there were also black people from across the diaspora. We could see women in hijab casually strolling the streets, and the house itself was near a small Jewish cemetery. It was five blocks from Lake Erie and the beach. We put in an offer and closed in July.

I had some guilt about leaving the Lexington neighborhood. I knew our buyer probably wouldn't be black and it came at a time when we heard that another empty-nester black couple was considering selling (they later changed their mind and stayed).

Were we leaving the neighborhood better than we found it? I wasn't sure. We were definitely leaving it more expensive than before. And a couple of the new neighbors weren't really into the community feel that the block had when we moved in. New neighbors were all white and kept to themselves outside of brief hellos. Few of them seemed approachable about watching your house or dog if you left town, and high privacy fences cut down on backyard chatter. It seemed to be enough for new neighbors to say that they were on Johnson Avenue; some, but not all, of the newcomers displayed interest in maintaining the type of contact and communication that had made the block so great in the first place.

Detroit-Shoreway gave me feelings of deja vu. Physically, it was "...[A] run of glossy new restaurants and boutiques on the old Hispanic strip, dotted in among the botanicas and social clubs, and the shuttered outlets full of dusty plastic furniture and out of date appliances. ... The street would be barely recognizable for how chic it had become." That was from *The Fortress of Solitude*, when Dylan returns to Boerum Hill for the first time in almost 15 years, but also applicable to our new neighborhood.

As in all the gentrifying areas I lived in, there is an emphasis on the precious: a soda fountain/ice cream shop named after the city's founder Moses Cleaveland with a sign at the register saying that in order to recreate a true, authentic 19th century soda fountain experience that service would be really, *really* slow; a small studio that offered naked yoga; theaters featuring work by Cleveland playwrights, art galleries, and boutique clothing stores mixed in with older businesses: diners, tattoo parlors, public library branches, and antique stores. Condos were going up near the walking path to the lake and I could see new directional signage branding the neighborhood and Gordon Square. It was culturally and architecturally historic; the elaborate 19th century Catholic churches were packed on Sundays with worshippers taking services in Spanish, German and Latin. I took my father to Mass one Sunday when he came to visit. Gentrification was happening fully on this side of town, as opposed to the mostly-black east side, where there were square miles of city blocks that looked like rural fields, still vacant after the 1966 Hough riots. But unlike most neighborhoods I had seen, these white people hadn't left the city when black people started moving in, likely because they couldn't afford to. The 2010 Census showed the area's poverty rate was 43 percent, compared with the city's overall rate of 31 percent.

Cleveland was affected by the triad of Big Bads like many other cities. The city is mostly segregated. There was a particularly nasty fight to integrate the public school system in 1963, during which a white pro-integration minister was crushed to death by a bulldozer and countless black protestors were beaten by mobs and police, arrested and jailed. Because of the city's geographic challenges between its east and west sides, which would have included crossing the river and highways, the schools never did desegregate in a way that would have brought true equality to the city's students. White and black people who could afford to do so decamped for suburban schools. In my neighborhood, public charter and religious schools seem to be the default; I saw a sign one day in the window of the organic juice bar advertising a new location of an exclusive private school to be built in the neighborhood for "West Side families." I imagined that if the school were for *all* West Side families, a flyer would have also been placed at the butcher shop or the Puerto Rican restaurant on Detroit Avenue, written in español. The flyer's location at the juice bar communicated exactly what and to whom it meant to communicate.

The area was subjected to redlining, likely due to the high numbers of immigrants, as there were few black families living on the west side in the 20th century. New Deal-era Home Owners' Loan Corporation maps, which were color-coded by banks and realtor organizations to determine credit ratings, showed Detroit-Shoreway as red, a grade of "Hazardous," or the lowest rating possible. A HOLC report written in 1939 said the majority of residents were a mix of European immigrants. The neighborhood was one percent black, and a note on the second page of the report revealed that "there was a small Colored settlement in the northeast part of this area, but there (sic) homes were razed for the Main Avenue Bridge and also for the Slum Clearance Project."

Additionally, the report noted that "Proximity to Public Square and to industry and because of convenience to transportation, schools, stores, churches, etc., this area will remain attractive to these type of occupants." The low HOLC ratings affected the pre-gentrification property values for decades and explains why I'm currently seeing lots and homes in the neighborhood snatched up and flipped within a matter of weeks. In the present day, language from realtors on websites like Zillow or Realtor.com suggests that they are trying to attract young, white couples, with and without children. Nothing I've seen specifically speaks to immigrants or people of color.

As far as law enforcement, I was aware of Cleveland policing before I moved there; we live less than two miles from where 12-year-old Tamir Rice was killed by police in 2015 while playing in a park, and the Justice Department's subsequent consent decree speaks to a documented need to change the culture of policing in the city.[42] It's on my mind when people at the block club meetings start talking about calling the police over petty concerns. One day, while at the Cleveland Public Library with my sons, I saw my then 2-year-old son pick up a plastic banana from the toy bin and start pointing it like a weapon. My flight or fight response kicked in and without being consciously aware of what I was doing, I leapt over and snatched it out of his hands. Tamir was killed over a toy. I think about it all the time.

Cleveland Mayor Frank Jackson, who was elected in 2007 and re-elected in 2017, released a report after the election titled *Making Cleveland a Community of Choice*. The report was also a blueprint for a long-term plan of economic development by 2020. The report uses many of the ideas and lingo that developers and city planners are trying to use to bring certain people back into the city: *walkable, diverse, transit, sustainable, parks and public spaces*. It champions the "eds and meds" strategy that Baltimore and other cities have utilized, hoping to capitalize on the Cleveland Clinic and various colleges like Cleveland State University and Case Western Reserve University on the east side of the city.[43]

The city developed what it calls the "neighborhood market typology," that categorizes housing into five types: regional choice (prime); stable (good condition and desirable); transitional (moderate housing values, needs rehabilitation); fragile (areas of low property value); distressed (lots of demolition or abandonment, don't build residential areas here). Detroit-Shoreway was rated as a mix of Stable or Regional Choice and Transitional/Fragile. The analysis leading to those recommendations was based on maps created at the Census Block Group level. Areas that were redlined for decades on the HOLC are nearly an exact overlay for the CBG maps. The report also suggests that homes in transitional areas may be subject to "aggressive demolition" if they can't be rehabbed for a decent cost.

How can we ever hope to move forward if we are only making choices from the same old template?

There's nothing inherently wrong with preserving old buildings with unique characteristics, just like it's not a bad thing to reduce greenhouse gases by encouraging communities that are near mass transit or encouraging people to walk to school or work. But where is the model that lets everyone do this equally? When will we stop trying to build on the dust of lies, omissions and violence?

CHAPTER 11

SUPERHEROES AMONG US

Let My People Grow!
(Superman #338)

Living in Cleveland, especially after living in Milwaukee and Chicago, is familiar, like opening a closet and seeing a dress I'd forgotten about and realizing that it still fits. The people, also products of the Great Migration, are my people, and I also understand how to move through northern urban spaces as a black woman more than I did in a city like Lexington. I feel strongly about situating myself within the historical context of the city, and not necessarily trying to make it fit my individual needs, which means respecting the superheros who have been doing the heavy lifting in Cleveland throughout periods of decline, of planned shrinkage, of unemployment and anti-black police violence, through a gutting and takeover of its public school system. The activists who are both insider and outsider; this is their home, but they refuse to participate in a system that isn't about truth and justice for everyone.

I take inspiration, for instance, from the United Freedom Movement, which started its own neighborhood freedom schools in response to the segregation of Cleveland Public Schools in the mid-1960s, and managed to unite black civil rights groups across class lines; or people like Mansfield Frazier, a former inmate turned radio host who created a biocellar as a model for green living and started his own vineyard, Chateau Hough, in the shadows of a riot-damaged neighborhood, employing other returning citizens on the site; or institutions like the historic Karamu House theater, which has been in its east side location for 100 years as the oldest black theater company in the country, offering a diverse range of programming for the city's youth. Efforts and institutions like these are what could push Cleveland beyond these same old cycles of segregation and economic inequality to truly become a city of tomorrow, the type of place in which people come to build community because of their differences, not in spite of them.

Cleveland Plain Dealer columnist Phillip Morris said in a May 2017 editorial that Cleveland's "forgotten parts" could use more superheroes though, especially on the east side, in black neighborhoods like Hough and Glenville. "Yes we're able to attract impressive investments in our downtown…and a smattering of West Side neighborhoods. What about the vast portions of the rest of Cleveland that continue to collapse under the weight of abandonment, joblessness and crime, not to mention car-swallowing potholes?" Morris pointed to Jerry Siegel's home on the east side, a well-maintained house in the middle of blight. "It seems to represent hope."

The thing about Morris' column, while true from a political or policy standpoint (he also pointed to the need for jobs in the community), is that it erases the people who have been there all this time, who have been doing their part to keep some type of community in place, whether they lobbied their councilman for a new grocery store in their neighborhood, or simply planted flowers in their garden year after year, keeping the faith that something can grow in a place marked as barren. If a tree can grow in Brooklyn, it can grow on the east side of Cleveland, too.

We never see Dylan reach this kind of growth, mostly because throughout the book, he remains in flight, on the run from his past, searching for authenticity, community, home. It's never really clear if he makes a true peace with his history, if he finds a true fortress of solitude. He finds Mingus, but since Mingus is imprisoned literally, it's as if the truth of Dylan's identity is also locked away. He also finds Rachel and faces his abandonment, but closure isn't peace.

What would Dylan be like now, seeing his old neighborhood no longer in flux but a fully affluent borough, more popular than Manhattan? Maybe he would have simply moved into his old home, as he would have likely inherited it from Abraham. Would he be sending his child to a magnet school, or Brooklyn Friends, as Isabel Vendle hinted at all those years ago? Or would he, like Nikole Hannah-Jones and her husband, decide on a neighborhood public school, leaving it an experience for his child to navigate as he did? Would he join the block club? Would he, anticipating a yoking, cross the street when approaching a group of black youth? What would Dylan be like if he'd addressed his past enough to contemplate a future that included having his own family?

Being a a black person in a gentrifying neighborhood can't just be about begging to have one's humanity recognized while buying craft donuts from a pop-up vendor. Or at least, I need for my life to be about more. My family and I recognize that as black people it can be meaningful to take up space in the city in places that white people are claiming for themselves—to return to an area in which black families were removed for a bridge. But it also means supporting the people who never left. It means making a commitment to neighborhood public schools even if you don't have kids, and advocating for affordable or low-income housing options. It means not calling the police over quality of life issues that you could simply knock on the door and speak to a neighbor about. It means eschewing NIMBYism and leaning into the discomfort of sharing space with people who aren't like you. It means lobbying elected officials at all levels for policy changing and funding that could mitigate or reverse the decades of racism and disinvestment.

Much of what Dylan experiences or embodies throughout *The Fortress of Solitude* is fear. Fear of rejection, of abandonment, of change. And I won't lie, I've been scared too. The history I carry with me and the skin I live in have conditioned me to be wary as well.

I know that no matter how many social identities I can slip on or through that I'm never safe from other people's best (or worst) intentions. Those same feelings of fear or trepidation are woven into the issues that affect or cause gentrification. We segregate because we are scared. Institutional segregation is built around white supremacy. The roots of that despicable garden sprout everything else, such as social policies and our refusal to talk to each other. We create gentrifying neighborhoods by using "diversity" as a selling point but cross the street or lock a car door if a black or Latinx person approaches.

We have to *see* each other. And see each other's humanity. Generally, people want the same things: to live somewhere safe; to raise kids (if they have them) in places they think are safe; to eat food that is fresh; to have access to equally funded education; to afford the roof over their head with jobs that pay living wages; to live without fear of harassment. Getting hung up on the fear of people who you think are outsiders: low-income people, people of color, disabled people, or immigrants and refusing to dialogue with them simply aggravates existing inequalities and carries fatal risks. That kind of fear turns all of our neighborhoods into tiny little fortresses and we become the soldiers who stand guard against anyone getting in.

This is how we lose, and how our stories become lies that repeat over in a never-ending cycle.

I want to know how we can win. And live together, with respect for each other's humanity.

CHAPTER 12

TALKING TO STRANGERS

"For decades the governing law of our cities has been 'Never speak to strangers.' I propose that in a democratic city, it is imperative that we speak to strangers, live next to them, and learn how to relate to them on many levels, from the political to the sexual."

—SAMUEL DELANY, *Times Square Red, Times Square Blue*

The Never-Ending Battle
(Superman: The Man of Steel Annual #5)

Over time, I've been as transient as Dylan, which has allowed me to observe many things, but being able to truly settle down as a useful member of the community has been challenging. My social mobility has also expressed itself through movement, and class privilege combined with a lack of dependents throughout my

20s and early 30s allowed and in some cases mandated that I move to different parts of the country to further my career, first as a journalist, then as a librarian/archivist. While on the move, I witnessed some truly inspiring or powerful displays of community building: Cabrini-Green residents in Chicago who created their own political advocacy organizations to fight their removal; or the Boston Latinx and Caribbean residents who fought hard to stop the closing of the Hi-Lo Food Market in Jamaica Plain in 2011, knowing that the Whole Foods to come in its place would signal the true end to a mixed-income neighborhood.

My Johnson Avenue neighbors in Lexington, the original ones we met when we moved into that corner duplex in 2012, were the oft-referred-to "village" that everyone claims is missing from today's communities. They taught me what being neighborly looked like. The city's Vice Mayor, Steve Kay and his wife Rona Roberts, and activist Tanya Torp host separate community meals in their homes, open to anyone in the neighborhood. Guests could be local business owners or they could be people who are homeless and struggling with addiction who are in need of a meal. There were people in that Lexington who showed me what a neighborhood could really be if people unselfconsciously opened themselves up to each other's possibilities. That was instructive; I had to learn how to be a good neighbor, learn how to really talk to others and open myself up to the full range of humanity around me. We don't have to be alien to each other. The ways that Dylan and I separately move through the world, or even Kal-El, as the sum of our multiple selves, colliding into obstacles as we attempt to search for a place that we can be at home—they're no different from the ways in which everyone else moves through the world, grasping and yearning, for the ability to be at home with themselves and with everyone else.

Dylan discovered that Thomas Wolfe was right, that you really can't go home again. People whom he only remembered from a single point in time moved on, got old, weren't interested in living in the past as he had done. He couldn't even deal with Mingus as an adult. The neighborhood is not static either. New people, buildings made new through renovation, new commerce, new problems.

Gentrification relies on nostalgia and people's affinity for certain types of history. A May 2017 *Washington Post* article described Derek Hyra's theory of "black branding," which draws white people into formerly black neighborhoods with residential buildings named for famous, historically relevant black artists and intellectuals, like musician Duke Ellington or writer Langston Hughes.[44] The new residents love the idea of the history but won't engage with anyone who physically embodies that past.

The nostalgia is a trap. Things can never be what they were because they were never what they appeared to be in the first place. Dylan's white, male body and social status as an adult will always give him cover, even if 50 kids yell "play that funky music whiteboy" at him. As a black woman, I don't want to move backward to any point in time in this American history. None of it is good. There are times when the present looks grim while walking in my skin.

We can't move backward to how our communities used to be either. Technology has changed the texture of our interactions too dramatically, and it's unlikely that millennials or anyone who comes after them will return to a pre-Internet way of building relationships, in or out of their neighborhoods. In Marc J. Dunkelman's book *The Vanishing Neighbor: The Transformation of American Community*, he noted that "social networking sites like Facebook and Twitter have more recently made it possible for Americans to benefit from collective action without even shaking hands with their peers." It also has allowed us to self-segregate even more than before.

Social networking sites are where we tell everyone who we are and what we value. We create digital communities of like-minded peers and often do not step outside of that. A section of Dunkelman's book, written in 2014, eerily prophesized what happened after the 2016 presidential election, which saw people arguing over the effects of Facebook, and the idea that we had so cloistered ourselves within our online communities and groups, listening to our own echo chambers of people who thought exactly as we did that a lot of people were absolutely shocked that Trump won the White House. I'm certain that an adult Dylan, who probably remembered Trump in 1980s New York, would have been perplexed, too. Too many Democrats or liberals only listened to other liberals online. It never occurred to them that there were millions of people who earnestly subscribed to The Lie.

Our real-life neighborhoods and physical interactions have changed because we have disrupted those options with technology, in segregated and integrated communities. Where Dylan had few choices to play outside of his neighborhood back in the day—Rachel Ebdus would not have set up play dates with someone in a Facebook progressive moms group—now people are meeting online and bridging the distance with each other. It's possible to set up a play date with someone who lives across town because of a shared Pinterest-recipe connection versus knocking on a neighbor's door and letting kids play close to home. Groceries can be ordered and delivered, Amazon can ship desired goods to the front door. As Dunkelman says, "the circumstances that once compelled Americans to develop the sort of familiar but less intimate relationships that were a staple of postwar American life have faded.... And while there's nothing wrong with that per se, we ought not to be so naive as to think that those new relationships don't come at a cost." In this way, we're not really building a community with each other. We're just back in our fortresses, truly in solitude, on guard against anything in the world that might be different.

Things don't have to be how they were in the past. And they don't have to stay as they are in the present, with us even more separated and afraid of each other. All kinds of people are trying to change that. Living in diverse, dynamic urban settings is about more than, say loaning a cup of sugar or a few eggs, though it can look like that. I was able to borrow a couple of eggs from a neighbor my first couple of weeks in Cleveland, as I didn't have as many as I thought but I had three hungry kids expecting pancakes. These days, it also means being aware of and responsive to the socioeconomic or racial issues that predate anyone's arrival. I would think a good neighbor is someone who doesn't call the police over a guy urinating in the alley. Especially if that guy is a person of color. A good neighbor may be someone who grows fruits and veggies in their yard, with a sign that tells others to help themselves.

Months after my first Cleveland block club meeting, the friendly block club president who'd shown annoyance with Angry Man's racism held a summer potluck at his home and invited everyone. It was a gorgeous day and everyone was friendly, the beer and the heat loosened all tongues. People introduced themselves and I that realized my family and I were no longer the newcomers. Even more people had arrived since we got there. But since I didn't get the same guarded vibe that I usually do when I arrive as a black woman to such events, everyone just started talking to each other like human beings. We talked honestly and without tension or defensiveness about housing discrimination and public schools. I found out that Angry Man had pissed off some of the other residents, both recent and established. But some of the more veteran members of the neighborhood felt positive they could turn his attitude around and get him to appreciate the diversity of Detroit-Shoreway. Delano and I left the party when the kids started getting restless, but we felt more hopeful than we had in a while that perhaps we had a village here too that we could be a part of.

The Participatory City, edited by Yasminah Beebeejaun, has various examples of the ways in which we can build our urban communities to be equitable for everyone. Muki Haklay's essay on "participatory sensing," or using mobile devices and data toward apps and programs that will encourage environmental justice in the urban environment, like testing air quality or detecting potholes, is one example. Haklay acknowledges the socio-economic and accessibility barriers to mobile device use, suggesting that underserved users should serve on the usability and data collection teams, so that everyone is engaged in some part of the process.

Artists in different cities are claiming space with public works or performance to draw attention to the erasure of people and communities caused by gentrification. Philadelphia attorney Rasheedah Phillips is a housing justice attorney and afrofuturist writer who developed what she calls the Community Futures Lab—a center that actively encourages residents in North Philadelphia to create oral histories about the neighborhood. The Community Futures Lab also offers different classes on everything from yoga to housing justice to zine collecting. Given that it's an exercise in futurism, neighbors are encouraged to share not just memories, but thoughts on what they want to see happen in years to come. Another example is Hume Chicago, a community-led art and programming space for underserved residents in the Humboldt Park and Logan Square neighborhoods, both of which are facing rapid gentrification.

The theory of experiemics, as explored in *Socially Restorative Urbanism* by Kevin Thwaites, Alice Mathers and Ian Simkins, also presents a cogent way to conceptualize urban living. Experiemics breaks down our relationship to the environment starting with how we position ourselves in that environment through language. We have territorial relationships to space through phrases such as *mine, theirs, ours,* or *yours*. These phrases, depending on how we relate to them or where we categorize ourselves, are things that can impede public participation and conversation— the two things needed most to try and help break down our barriers. By interrogating and breaking down the language, we could move into more localized and participatory expressions of community, ones that allow more people across a variety of identities to contribute and be heard. Experiemics is a concept that could take a sledgehammer to The Lie, not by omitting it or erasing its existence, but by altering the concept of land "ownership" in such a way that is inclusive of everyone.

The book focuses its case study on a community of people with learning disabilities in the United Kingdom, as an example of a community frequently left out of conversations about gentrification or city planning in general, and the study emphasizes that underrepresented groups have traditionally been the least likely to participate in placemaking and urban planning because of their systemic exclusion and not a lack of interest. The researchers engaged the community for their input on a city park, recognizing green space as an "ours" entity that is socially desirable and beneficial to all, but one that can also be designed with different accessibility points for different users.

After getting feedback from the group, the researchers, facilitated partnerships with a film production company so that members of the community could express in their own words the meaning of the park to them and for everyone else who would be able to use it. It's a radically inclusive model we could look to for a variety of urban issues and would help engage those of us who are outsiders in various settings, to melt away the gap between "mine" and "yours" in our urban spaces.

The thing about *The Fortress of Solitude* that I come back to, is that it's not that being an outsider is the worst thing. It's that we treat it like it is. At the end of the book, Dylan is still himself, he hasn't changed or become less awkward. And that's okay. My story hasn't ended. I'm still a black woman with varying levels of social mobility that can get me into places, but once I'm in the room, there's no telling how any interaction will go. One thing that remains the same for both me and Dylan is that there's no walls that can hold you up or keep you safe from the outside world if you're not at home with yourself, whoever that person is. The problems in our neighborhoods and communities have no time for inauthenticity. It serves no one to hold on to The Lie, or the series of lies we tell to make ourselves comfortable. We can fight a lot of things together if we can fight that fear that keeps us apart.

Maybe, to paraphrase Audre Lorde, we are the superheroes we've been waiting for. And if so, we have the power to change our futures, like Rasheedah Phillips suggests. We can change the stories we've been buying into for so long and start with the truth as the way forward. Dylan doesn't get there. But I have to. I have no choice.

ENDNOTES

1   Calimani, Riccardo. *The Ghetto of Venice*. Italy: Oscar Mondadori, 2001.

2   Yusef Salaam, Anton McCray, Raymond Santana, Kevin Richardson, and Korey Wise—teenagers at the time of their arrest—were later freed when serial rapist Matias Reyes confessed to the crime while incarcerated on other charges. They had served between six and 13 years before being released. In 2013, Mayor-elect Bill DiBlasio agreed to settle for $41 million a civil lawsuit the men filed against the city for wrongful imprisonment, among other charges.

3   Drug Abuse Resistance Education

4   Lethem's Camden College cohort is a direct nod to the affluent, nihilistic characters of Bret Easton Ellis' characters in *The Rules of Attraction*, one of whom is the brother of Patrick Bateman, the lead of Easton Ellis' '80s satire *American Psycho*.

5   Levine, Marc. "The Crisis of Black Male Joblessness in Milwaukee: Trends, Policies, and Policy Options. *Center for Economic Development.* University of Wisconsin at Milwaukee, 2007. www4.uwm.edu/ced/publications/blackcrisis307.pdf

6   Historic Designation Study Report: Albert P. Kunzelmann House. Published by the City of Milwaukee, 2007. www.city.milwaukee.gov/ImageLibrary/Groups/cityHPC/DesignatedReports/vticnf/HDKunzelmann.pdf

7 Full disclosure, I now work for the University of Chicago Libraries as of August 2018.

8 Vale, Lawrence. "Housing Chicago: From Cabrini-Green to Parkside of Old Town." *Places Journal.* February 01, 2012. www.placesjournal.org/article/housing-chicago-cabrini-green-to-parkside-of-old-town/.

9 Channick, Robert. "Mark Twain Hotel to Be Renovated under SRO Preservation Ordinance." Chicagotribune.com. June 01, 2016. www.chicagotribune.com/business/ct-single-room-occupancy-hotel-redevelopment-0531-biz-20160527-story.html.

10 "Growing Our City, Promoting Our Farms." Fayette Alliance. fayettealliance.com/.

11 Eads, Morgan. "Lexington Is the Country's Third Least Diverse Large City, According to Recent Study." *Lexington Herald-Leader.* Kentucky.com. February 22, 2017. www.kentucky.com/news/local/counties/fayette-county/article134236844.html.

12 "Among Single Baby Boomers, White Men Possess 160 Percent Greater Wealth than Women of Color." Institute for Women's Policy Research. February 16, 2017. iwpr.org/among-single-baby-boomers-white-men-possess-160-greater-wealth-women-color/.

13 Maksim, Hanja. Bergman, Manfred Max. "Residential Location, Mobility and the City," *Mobilities and Inequality.* Surrey: Ashgate Publishing Limited, 2009.

14 A recent book by Daniel Hyra, *Race, Class, and Politics in the Cappucino City* (University of Chicago Press, 2017) discussed an idea of "living the wire," the concept that white people were choosing to live in certain areas of Washington, D.C., because of the areas' proximity to crime, and using it as social currency at cocktail parties

15 Fort, Ellen. "UPDATED: Doughp, SF's 'Hip-Hop-Inspired' Cookie Dough Kiosk, Inspires Backlash." *Eater SF*. September 19, 2017. sf.eater.com/2017/9/19/16334700 /doughp-cookie-dough-scoops-san-francisco.

16 Krysan M, Couper MP, Farley R, Forman T. "Does Race Matter in Neighborhood Preferences? Results from a Video Experiment." *American Journal of Sociology*. 2009; 115(2):527-559.

17 Eligon, John and Robert Gebeloff. "Segregation, the Neighbor That Won't Leave." *New York Times*. August 21, 2017. A1-A12.

18 Eblen, Tom. "North Limestone Group Gets $550,000 Grant to Help Turn Bus Station into Public Market." *Lexington Herald-Leader*. Kentucky.com. www.kentucky.com/news /local/news-columns-blogs/tom-eblen/article44565990.html

19 Hannah-Jones, Nikole. "Worlds Apart: Choosing a School for my Daughter in a Segregated City." *New York Times Magazine*. June 9, 2016.

20 I worked in the Special Collections Research Center at the University of Kentucky between 2013–2016.

21 "Globe Spotlight: Shadow Campus, Part 1: Boston's Broken Student Housing System." *The Boston Globe*. BostonGlobe .com. May 04, 2014. www.bostonglobe.com/metro/2014 /05/03/allston-fire-overcrowded-house-takes-promising -student-life/THC5c82P53NQdsSAETKurK/story.html.

22 Sun, Julie Scharper. "Baltimore Colleges Push to Improve Neighborhoods." *Baltimore Sun*. Baltimoresun.com. January 14, 2013. www.baltimoresun.com/news/maryland/baltimore -city/bs-md-ci-anchor-universities-20130112-story.html

23 2013-2014 Civil Rights Data Collection, U.S. Department of Education, Office of Civil Rights.

24 Freddie Gray

25 Samuel Dubose

26 Tony Robinson

27 Mapping Police Violence puts the number of unarmed African Americans murdered by police at 102 in 2015. Mapping Police Violence. mappingpoliceviolence.org/unarmed/.

28 This was before Sandra Bland, Korryn Gaines, Tanisha Anderson, and Rekia Boyd.

29 "AT&T's Digital Redlining Of Cleveland." National Digital Inclusion Alliance. March 17, 2017. https://digitalinclusion.org/blog/2017/03/10/atts-digital-redlining-of-cleveland/.

30 Butler, Bethonie. "'Sesame Street' Says Goodbye to Gordon, Bob and Luis. Fans Are Not Happy." *The Washington Post*. August 02, 2016. www.washingtonpost.com/news/arts-and-entertainment/wp/2016/07/28/sesame-street-says-goodbye-to-gordon-bob-and-luis-fans-are-not-happy/?utm_term=.59cb1e3119b6

31 Petrovic, Ana "The elderly facing gentrification: neglect, invisibility, entrapment, and loss." *The Elder Law Journal*. 2008, Vol. 15, p. 534.

32 Seidel, Jon. "Con Man Targeted Elderly Homeowners in $10M Scam, Feds Say." *Chicago Sun-Times*. May 23, 2017. chicago.suntimes.com/news/con-man-targeted-elderly-homeowners-in-10m-scam-feds-say/.

33 Full disclosure, I had an internship at the Jim Henson Company in New York in 2011. The location in Long Island City, Queens, is also where the Muppets for Sesame Street are created.

34 Roberts, Sam. "Moynihan in His Own Words." *The New York Times*. September 19, 2010. http://www.nytimes.com/2010/09/20/nyregion/20moynihan.html. Moynihan later claimed that his comments were misinterpreted and that benign neglect or urban disinvestment wasn't a policy suggestion, though given his position as President Richard

Nixon's urban affairs adviser, his words had considerable impact and were used as justification for planned shrinkage policies in urban, low-income black communities all over the country. Planned shrinkage, which was meant to cover lost tax revenue from white flight, decreased city services like garbage removal or sewer maintenance, and police and fire in neighborhoods blighted by riots and crime.

35 Maxey-Boyd, Alva Beatrice. "Finding Aid." Chicago Public Library, Vivian G. Harsh Research Collection, Woodson Regional Library.

36 Twelve-year-old Tamir Rice, killed by Cleveland police after a 911 call that complained about the boy playing with a toy gun in the park. The caller identified the gun as a toy; the 911 dispatcher failed to relay that information to responding officers, who jumped out of their car and shot him without even announcing themselves.

37 Coleman, Jonny. "How These Wooden Fences Became a Symbol of Gentrification Across Los Angeles." *LAist.* May 4, 2016. http://laist.com/2016/05/04/wooden_slat_fences.php.

38 Andreou, Alex. "Defensive Architecture: Keeping Poverty Unseen and Deflecting Our Guilt." *The Guardian.* February 18, 2015. https://www.theguardian.com/society/2015/feb/18 /defensive-architecture-keeps-poverty-undeen-and-makes-us -more-hostile.

39 "Cleveland, the True Birthplace of Superman." Smithsonian .com. August 18, 2010. www.smithsonianmag.com/arts -culture/cleveland-the-true-birthplace-of-superman -56671378/.

40 The Siegel & Shuster Society. http://supermanincleveland .com/news.html.

41 "The Time Superman and Batgirl Went On A Blind Date." Slay, Monstrobot of the Deep!! http://slaymonstrobot.blogspot .com/2011/01/time-superman-and-batgirl-went-on-blind .html.

42 Full disclosure: In 2015, before I moved to Cleveland, I along with other members of the Society of American Archivists began volunteering on an oral history and archiving project in partnership with Cleveland activist group Puncture the Silence called A People's Archive of Police Violence in Cleveland, which is a collection of interviews and primary source documents contributed by people who have either experienced police violence personally or want to comment on the situation in general. I currently serve on the Archivist Advisory Board for the project, and we've continued to collect additional materials. www.archivingpoliceviolence.org/

43 I was employed by Case Western Reserve University as a librarian from March 2017 to July 2018.

44 McCartney, Robert. "'Black Branding'—How a D.C. Neighborhood Was Marketed to White Millennials." *The Washington Post*. May 03, 2017. www.washingtonpost.com /local/black-branding--how-a-dc-neighborhood-was-marketed -to-white-millenials/2017/05/02/68b0ae06-2f47-11e7-9534 -00e4656c22aa_story.html?utm_term=.523d132f02cc.

ACKNOWLEDGMENTS

I can do all things through God and jazz music that are possible. Thank you Brian Hurley for helping me refine my writing at The Rumpus and now with this book. You helped me expand my understanding of what literary criticism could be and gave me the opportunity to share it. Catapult editors Mensah Demary and Morgan Jerkins, for being so open and accessible and, in your separate ways, helping me interrogate my stories. Nicole Fonsh and Steven Booth for being the best readers. Always Myrna Morales for whispering in my ear the things that I need to know. Jonathan Lethem for writing *The Fortress of Solitude* and giving me something to come back to again and again. My family for the unwavering love and support that gave me the time and opportunity needed to make sense of everything. And to Delano, my Superman. We could live anywhere in the universe, but your heart is my home.